# COOKING FROM
# FROZEN
### IN YOUR INSTANT POT®

## 100 Foolproof Recipes with No Thawing

## KRISTY BERNARDO

Author of *Weeknight Cooking With Your Instant Pot®*
and founder of The Wicked Noodle

**PHOTOGRAPHY BY BECKY WINKLER**

PAGE STREET
PUBLISHING CO.

PAGE STREET
PUBLISHING CO.

First published in 2018 by
Page Street Publishing Co.
27 Congress Street, Suite 105
Salem, MA 01970
www.pagestreetpublishing.com

Distributed by Macmillan, sales in Canada by The Canadian Manda Group.

22  21 20 19 18   1 2 3 4 5

ISBN-13: 978-1-62414-682-4
ISBN-10: 1-62414-682-1

Library of Congress Control Number: 2018948766

Cover and book design by Laura Gallant and Meg Baskis for Page Street Publishing Co.
Photography copyright © 2018 by Becky Winkler

Printed and bound in the United States

Instant Pot® is a registered trademark of Double Insight, Inc., which was not involved in the creation of this book.

FOR MY GIRLS,
KYLIE + KATIE

# CONTENTS

# INTRODUCTION

When I was growing up, we had a freezer in our basement that was filled with meat at the beginning of winter and would dwindle down as spring approached. Much of that meat was venison from the fall hunting season, but my mom was also a frugal shopper who would stock up when meat was on sale. There was almost always some meat defrosting in the sink when I walked in the door from school, which usually saved my mom from having to hear "What's for dinner?" repeatedly.

Flash forward a few years (I won't say just how many!) and now I fill my own freezer with meats I find at a good price. I also love to pick up meat in bulk at Costco, but it's almost always too much for me to cook at once, so into the freezer goes whatever is left. I'm not quite as diligent about keeping tabs on it as my mom was, however, so every couple of years when I'm cleaning it out I'll invariably find a few roasts that I can't quite identify anymore. I know I'm not alone in this! Planning ahead to unthaw something that morning or the night before doesn't happen as often as we'd like.

But the Instant Pot changes all that.

You will love putting something frozen and unrecognizable into your Instant Pot, closing the lid and seeing it magically transformed into a delicious meal when you open it back up! The meat gets incredibly tender and you won't be able to tell the difference from a roast that's never been frozen before. The Instant Pot will simplify the way you cook, and starting with frozen meats and vegetables will make your life that much easier.

This book starts with mainly frozen meats, but I've also included some recipes that utilize other frozen ingredients, such as frozen pasta, vegetables and even fruit. And now, instead of an overflowing freezer that has gotten away from me, mine gets used almost every day! I'm confident it will do the same for you and your family.

*K Bernardo*

# TIPS FOR COOKING FROM FROZEN IN YOUR INSTANT POT

**BEFORE FREEZING**

Keep the shape and size of your Instant Pot in mind before freezing meats. You may need to cut or arrange your meat before freezing to ensure you can just pop it into the pot.

Separate individual pieces, such as chicken breasts or thighs, so that they won't stick together once frozen. Large blocks of meats that are stuck together take much longer to cook.

I used both large- and small-sized chicken breasts in these recipes and didn't notice a difference in the end result, even when the cooking times remained the same. As long as the pieces go into the pot individually rather than all stuck together in a frozen block (see prior paragraph), the meat will cook beautifully.

Divide larger cuts of meat, such as roasts, into two to four pieces. Large cuts of meat won't cook as well as smaller pieces, even if it's all cooked at the same time.

If you happen to have fresh meats on hand, you can still make these recipes; however, the time under pressure will need to be reduced. For chicken, reduce the time by 2 minutes. For larger roasts, reduce by 10 minutes.

**AFTER FREEZING**

If you must put a block of meat, such as chicken breasts, into the pot, and find that they're not completely cooked after cooking at pressure, you can place the uncooked side into the liquid in the pot and switch to "Saute" mode, essentially finishing the cooking in the poaching liquid. This will also work if you start with unfrozen meats.

Shrimp is extremely easy to overcook. When in doubt, always go with the lowest setting and, if needed, gently finish cooking after.

Keep in mind that starting with frozen meats means that it will take your Instant Pot slightly longer to come to pressure. On average, I noticed a 10-minute increase, so please keep that in mind when planning dinnertime.

I used a 6-quart (5.7-L) Instant Pot for all of the recipes in this book. Anything larger will also work; however, if your Instant Pot is 5 quarts (4.7 L) or smaller, adjustments may be needed.

A few of the sandwich recipes call for leaving the meat on the counter for 30 minutes to soften. You don't want to thaw the meat entirely, but soften it just enough so that it's easier to get thin slices. Alternatively, if you're starting with fresh meat, freeze the meat for 30 minutes to achieve the same effect.

You may notice that a few recipes call for browning the meat directly from the freezer with the "Saute" setting. If you've never done this before, don't worry—it works incredibly well! The meat browns up beautifully, does not burn, and it turns out a great piece of meat when finished with the "Manual" pressure setting.

# CHICKEN DINNERS IN A FLASH

Chicken is typically what fills my freezer most. Our local grocer frequently has "Buy 2, Get 3 Free" specials, and I love to stock up when those deals hit. Since it's so versatile, it gets used in no time in our house. There's no cut of frozen chicken I've found that doesn't work well in the Instant Pot, making chicken my number one choice when buying in bulk. You can't beat the versatility of using frozen chicken for delicious, go-to family meals that turn out tender and juicy! This chapter includes a variety of flavorful chicken dishes your whole family will love.

## MY THREE FAVORITES
Indian Butter Chicken (page 12)
Blackened Chicken Thighs (page 27)
Cajun Chicken Alfredo (page 31)

# CHICKEN WITH LEMON AND CAPERS

This is my easier version of chicken piccata, but it's also better since the Instant Pot turns your frozen chicken into meat so tender it almost falls off the bone. If you like, you can make a side of angel hair pasta and it will taste almost identical!

**YIELD: 4 TO 6 SERVINGS**

2 tsp (10 ml) extra-virgin olive oil

3 cloves garlic, minced

¼ cup (60 ml) dry white wine

½ cup (118 ml) low-sodium chicken broth

2 tbsp (30 ml) fresh lemon juice

8 frozen bone-in, skin-on chicken thighs

3 tbsp (26 g) capers

1 tbsp (14 g) cold butter

2 tbsp (5 g) chopped fresh parsley

Press "Saute" to preheat your Instant Pot. When the word "Hot" appears on the display, add the oil. When the oil is shimmering, add the garlic and cook for about a minute. Add the wine and cook until it's reduced to a tablespoon (15 ml), about 5 minutes. Turn off the Instant Pot.

Add the chicken broth and lemon juice, then stir to scrape up all the browned bits from the bottom of the pot. Add the chicken to the pot, directly into the liquid.

Close and lock the lid of the Instant Pot. Press "Manual" and immediately adjust the timer to 30 minutes. Check that the cooking pressure is on "High" and that the release valve is set to "Sealing."

When the time is up, open the Instant Pot using "Quick Pressure Release." Remove the chicken and set it aside on a broiler pan. Remove the fat from the liquid in the pot, then stir in the capers, butter and parsley. Turn off the Instant Pot.

Broil the chicken until the skin is browned and crispy, for about 5 minutes. Top with the sauce and serve.

# INDIAN BUTTER CHICKEN

This is a favorite at our local Indian restaurant, but I love to make it in my Instant Pot too. The sauce has a wonderful flavor that is so good you'll want to drink it. It's slightly spicy, so feel free to reduce the amount of cayenne if you prefer.

**YIELD: 4 TO 6 SERVINGS**

2 tsp (10 ml) extra-virgin olive oil

¼ medium white onion, chopped

5 cloves garlic, minced

¼ tsp ground ginger (or 1 tbsp [14 g] fresh)

1 tsp paprika

1 tsp cayenne pepper

½ tsp ground coriander

1 tsp turmeric

2 tsp (5 g) garam masala

¼ cup (59 ml) chicken broth

2 lb (900 g) frozen boneless, skinless chicken breasts

1 (14.5-oz [411-g]) can diced tomatoes, with liquid

¼ cup (57 g) unsalted butter, cut into 8 pieces

½ cup (118 ml) heavy cream

1 large handful fresh cilantro, chopped

Cooked rice, for serving

Press "Saute" to preheat your Instant Pot. When the word "Hot" appears on the display, add the olive oil. When the oil is shimmering, add the onion and cook until it's soft, for about 5 minutes, stirring frequently. Add the garlic, ginger, paprika, cayenne, coriander, turmeric and garam masala and cook for 1 minute, stirring constantly. Turn off the Instant Pot.

Add the broth, stirring well to scrape up any browned bits from the bottom. Add the chicken, then pour the tomatoes on top; do not stir. Close and lock the lid of the Instant Pot. Press "Manual" and immediately adjust the timer to 10 minutes. Check that the cooking pressure is on "High" and that the release valve is set to "Sealing."

When the time is up, open the Instant Pot using "Quick Pressure Release" and remove the chicken to a cutting board to cool it slightly. Press "Cancel," then immediately press "Saute." Add the butter and cream; stir well. Using an immersion blender, puree the sauce until smooth.

Cut the chicken into bite-sized pieces and add it back to the pot to gently reheat. Stir in the cilantro. Serve over rice.

# WHOLE BLACKENED CHICKEN

Cooking a whole, frozen chicken in my Instant Pot is one of my favorite things to do! It's economical and my entire family loves it. It tastes just like roasting a chicken in the oven, but the meat gets very tender and juicy. If you prefer, you can shred the meat and toss it with a cup (240 ml) or so of the liquid to make delicious shredded chicken sandwiches. The rub on this chicken is perfect for spice lovers!

**YIELD: 4 SERVINGS**

1 tsp paprika

2 tsp (4 g) smoked paprika

¼ tsp cayenne pepper

½ tsp thyme

½ tsp oregano

½ tsp garlic powder

1 tsp onion powder

½ tsp coarse salt

½ tsp coarsely ground black pepper

4 cups (950 ml) water

1 medium onion, chopped

1 bay leaf

1 (3–4 lb [1.3–1.8 kg]) frozen chicken

Mix together the paprika, smoked paprika, cayenne pepper, thyme, oregano, garlic powder, onion powder, salt and pepper and set it aside.

Add the water, onion and bay leaf to your Instant Pot. Rub the chicken all over with the spice mixture, then place it in your Instant Pot, directly in the liquid. The chicken may not lie flat in the pot, but that's okay. It just needs to be placed inside, even if at a slight angle.

Close and lock the lid of the Instant Pot. Press "Manual" and immediately adjust the timer to 60 minutes. Check that the cooking pressure is on "High" and that the release valve is set to "Sealing."

When the time is up, allow the pressure to release naturally for 10 minutes, then open the Instant Pot using "Quick Pressure Release." Carefully remove the chicken and place it on a carving board. Carve the chicken, then place the pieces on a broiler pan, skin side up. Broil the chicken pieces for approximately 5 minutes, or until the skin is crisped to your liking.

# CRISPY GARLIC AND PAPRIKA CHICKEN THIGHS

Don't be fooled by the few ingredients in this recipe—it's packed with flavor! The chicken thighs turn out incredibly tender in the Instant Pot and a quick broil gives them crispy skin, as if you cooked them in the oven.

## YIELD: 4 SERVINGS

2 cups (472 ml) chicken broth or water

2 lb (900 g) frozen bone-in, skin-on chicken thighs

2 tbsp (14 g) paprika

2 tsp (4 g) garlic powder

¼ tsp coarse salt

1 tsp freshly ground black pepper

¼ cup (57 g) unsalted butter, melted

Add the chicken broth or water to the pot, then add the chicken thighs.

Close and lock the lid of the Instant Pot. Press "Manual" and immediately adjust the timer to 30 minutes. Check that the cooking pressure is on "High" and that the release valve is set to "Sealing."

When the time is up, open the Instant Pot using "Quick Pressure Release." Remove the chicken from the pot and place it on a broiler pan. Broil until the chicken is browned and crispy, for about 5 minutes.

Mix together the paprika, garlic powder, salt and pepper, then stir in the melted butter. Brush the thighs liberally with the butter mixture and serve immediately.

# WHOLE "ROTISSERIE" CHICKEN

I used to pick up a prepared rotisserie chicken from the grocery store at least once a week, but my Instant Pot changed all that! I love pulling a frozen bird from the freezer, cooking it in my Instant Pot and either eating it as-is, or using it in any number of recipes that call for cooked chicken.

**YIELD: 4 SERVINGS**

2 tsp (5 g) paprika

¼ tsp cayenne pepper

1 tsp thyme

¼ tsp oregano

1 tsp garlic powder

1 tsp onion powder

1 tbsp (8 g) coarse salt

1 tsp coarsely ground black pepper

4 cups (950 ml) water

1 medium onion, chopped

1 bay leaf

1 (3–4 lb [1.3–1.8 kg]) frozen chicken

Mix together the paprika, cayenne pepper, thyme, oregano, garlic powder, onion powder, salt and pepper and set it aside.

Add the water, onion and bay leaf to your Instant Pot.

Rub the chicken all over with the spice mixture, then place it in your Instant Pot, directly in the liquid.

Close and lock the lid of the Instant Pot. Press "Manual" and immediately adjust the timer to 60 minutes. Check that the cooking pressure is on "High" and that the release valve is set to "Sealing."

When the time is up, allow the pressure to release naturally for 10 minutes, then open the Instant Pot using "Quick Pressure Release." Carefully remove the chicken and place it on a carving board. Carve the chicken, then place the pieces on a broiler pan, skin side up. Broil the chicken pieces for approximately 5 minutes or until the skin is crisped to your liking. You can also broil the chicken whole if you prefer.

# BALSAMIC AND SWEET ONION CHICKEN

For so few ingredients, this recipe has incredible flavor. It's wonderful on its own with a vegetable side dish, or pile it onto a freshly toasted bun for a heavenly sandwich! I like to serve it with sugar snap peas and an extra drizzle of balsamic vinegar.

**YIELD: 4 SERVINGS**

2 tsp (10 ml) extra-virgin olive oil

1 large sweet onion, sliced

2 cloves garlic, minced

½ cup (120 ml) balsamic vinegar

¼ cup (59 ml) chicken broth

4 frozen boneless, skinless chicken breasts

1 tbsp (15 ml) honey

Coarse salt and freshly ground black pepper

Press "Saute" to preheat your Instant Pot. When the word "Hot" appears on the display, add the olive oil. When the oil is shimmering, add the onion. Cook until the onion is soft and starting to caramelize, for about 10 minutes, stirring frequently. Add the garlic and cook for 1 minute. Add the balsamic vinegar and chicken broth, stirring well to scrape up any browned bits from the bottom. Turn off the Instant Pot.

Add the chicken to the pot. Close and lock the lid of the Instant Pot. Press "Manual" and immediately adjust the timer to 10 minutes. Check that the cooking pressure is on "High" and that the release valve is set to "Sealing."

When the time is up, open the Instant Pot using "Quick Pressure Release." Remove the chicken from the pot and set it aside. Press "Cancel," then immediately press "Saute." Boil until the liquid in the pot is reduced and thickened, for about 5 minutes. Stir in the honey and season with salt and pepper to taste.

Slice the chicken breasts and place them on a platter or individual serving plates along with the onion mixture.

# LEMON-PEPPER CHICKEN WINGS

This wing recipe is incredibly popular with the readers of my food blog. I wasn't sure if it would work well in the Instant Pot, but the chicken turns out very tender and the skin crisps up well with a quick run under the broiler at the end. It's my daughter Kylie's favorite recipe, and she claims she likes the Instant Pot version best!

## YIELD: 4 SERVINGS

1 cup (236 ml) water or chicken broth

4 lb (1.8 kg) frozen chicken wings

¼ cup (57 g) butter, melted

2 tbsp (16 g) lemon-pepper seasoning

Add the water or chicken broth to the pot. Place a steamer basket into the Instant Pot and place the wings inside.

Close and lock the lid of the Instant Pot. Press "Manual" and immediately adjust the timer to 12 minutes. Check that the cooking pressure is on "High" and that the release valve is set to "Sealing."

When the time is up, open the Instant Pot using "Quick Pressure Release." Remove the chicken from the pot and place it on a broiler pan. Broil until the chicken is browned and crispy, for about 5 minutes.

Mix together the melted butter and lemon-pepper seasoning. Brush the wings with the butter mixture and serve immediately.

# ASIAN CHICKEN

I love this recipe because it starts not just with chicken from my freezer, but with pantry staples too, so I can make this dish quickly on a weeknight—with no running to the store. I like to serve this with sugar snap peas or mixed vegetables straight from my freezer (cooked according to the package directions).

## YIELD: 4 SERVINGS

½ cup (118 ml) chicken broth

¼ cup (59 ml) soy sauce

¼ cup (59 ml) rice wine vinegar

4 cloves garlic, minced

1½ tsp (3 g) ground ginger

¼ cup (36 g) brown sugar, loosely packed

4 frozen boneless, skinless chicken breasts

Cooked rice, for serving

Whisk together the broth, soy sauce, rice wine vinegar, garlic, ginger and brown sugar, then pour it into your Instant Pot. Add the chicken directly into the liquid.

Press "Manual" and immediately adjust the timer to 10 minutes. Check that the cooking pressure is on "High" and that the release valve is set to "Sealing."

When the time is up, open the Instant Pot using "Quick Pressure Release." Remove the chicken to a cutting board and cut it into slices. Serve the chicken and sauce over rice.

# CHICKEN WITH MUSTARD CREAM SAUCE

This creamy mustard sauce is so good you'll be licking your plate! Serve it with some sugar snap peas and mashed potatoes for the perfect quick meal.

**YIELD: 4 SERVINGS**

2 tsp (10 ml) extra-virgin olive oil

1 medium shallot, minced

2 cloves garlic, minced

¾ cup (177 ml) chicken broth

4 frozen boneless, skinless chicken breasts

2 sprigs fresh thyme

2 tbsp (30 ml) Dijon mustard

½ cup (118 ml) heavy cream

Course salt and freshly ground pepper

Press "Saute" to preheat your Instant Pot. When the word "Hot" appears on the display, add the olive oil.

When the oil is shimmering, add the shallot and sauté until it starts to soften, for about 5 minutes, stirring frequently. Add the garlic and cook for 1 minute. Turn off the Instant Pot.

Add the broth, stirring well to scrape up any browned bits from the bottom, then add the chicken. Close and lock the lid of the Instant Pot. Press "Manual" and immediately adjust the timer to 10 minutes. Check that the cooking pressure is on "High" and that the release valve is set to "Sealing."

When the time is up, open the Instant Pot using "Quick Pressure Release" and remove the chicken to a cutting board.

Press "Cancel," then immediately press "Saute." Add the thyme and boil the liquid until it's reduced by half, about 5 minutes, then stir in the Dijon and cream. Taste, then season with salt and pepper. Pour the sauce over the chicken and serve.

# CHICKEN WITH WHITE WINE AND HERB SAUCE

Your Instant Pot makes quick work of this flavorful, upscale chicken dish. The tarragon adds an unexpected flavor that makes it something special without any additional work. The sauce is perfect with rice or mashed potatoes as a side dish.

## YIELD: 4 SERVINGS

2 tsp (10 ml) extra-virgin olive oil

1 medium shallot, chopped

1 cup (236 ml) chicken broth

1 cup (236 ml) dry white wine

4 frozen boneless, skinless chicken breasts

½ cup (114 g) cold unsalted butter, cut into 8 pieces

2 tbsp (8 g) chopped parsley

2 tbsp (8 g) chopped tarragon

Coarse salt and freshly ground black pepper

Press "Saute" to preheat your Instant Pot. When the word "Hot" appears on the display, add the olive oil. When the oil is shimmering, add the shallot and cook until it starts to soften, for about 5 minutes, stirring frequently. Turn off the Instant Pot.

Add the broth and wine to the pot, then add the chicken. Close and lock the lid of the Instant Pot. Press "Manual" and immediately adjust the timer to 15 minutes. Check that the cooking pressure is on "High" and that the release valve is set to "Sealing."

When the time is up, open the Instant Pot using "Quick Pressure Release," then remove the chicken to a cutting board and allow it to cool slightly. Press "Cancel," then immediately press "Saute." Bring it to a boil and reduce the liquid by half, for about 5 to 7 minutes.

Add the butter, one piece at a time, stirring until it's melted and incorporated. Add the parsley and tarragon, taste, then season with salt and pepper.

Slice the chicken and place it back in the sauce to gently reheat.

# BLACKENED CHICKEN THIGHS

This blackening seasoning is one of the most popular recipes on my food blog. You may want to double or triple it and keep it in an airtight container so you can make these tender, juicy and flavorful thighs anytime, without having to mix the spices again. I make this recipe often because the chicken gets tender in a way the oven just can't match.

**YIELD: 4 SERVINGS**

2 cups (472 ml) chicken broth or water

2 lb (900 g) frozen bone-in chicken thighs

1 tsp paprika

2 tsp (4 g) smoked paprika

¼ tsp cayenne pepper

¼ tsp thyme

¼ tsp oregano

¼ tsp garlic powder

1 tsp onion powder

¼ tsp coarse salt

¼ tsp freshly ground black pepper

¼ cup (57 g) unsalted butter, melted

Add the chicken broth or water to the pot, then add the chicken thighs.

Close and lock the lid of the Instant Pot. Press "Manual" and immediately adjust the timer to 30 minutes. Check that the cooking pressure is on "High" and that the release valve is set to "Sealing."

When the time is up, open the Instant Pot using "Quick Pressure Release." Remove the chicken from the pot and place it on a broiler pan. Broil until the chicken is browned and crispy, for about 5 minutes.

Mix together the paprika, smoked paprika, cayenne, thyme, oregano, garlic powder, onion powder, salt and pepper, then stir in the melted butter. Brush the thighs liberally with the butter mixture and serve immediately.

# SALSA VERDE CHICKEN

This dish is delicious with a side of rice and refried beans for a complete Mexican-style meal. The rice will soak up the flavorful sauce wonderfully. If you're really in a rush, you can omit the fresh onion and garlic, skipping the first step altogether, and the salsa verde will still add plenty of flavor.

## YIELD: 6 SERVINGS

2 tsp (10 ml) extra-virgin olive oil

½ medium onion, chopped

2 cloves garlic, minced

½ cup (118 ml) chicken broth

1 (16-oz [453-g]) jar salsa verde

2 lb (900 g) frozen boneless, skinless chicken breasts

Coarse salt and freshly ground black pepper

1 cup (112 g) shredded Monterey Jack cheese

1 cup (112 g) shredded pepper jack cheese

¼ cup (10 g) chopped cilantro

Press "Saute" to preheat your Instant Pot. When the word "Hot" appears on the display, add the olive oil. When the oil is shimmering, add the onion and cook until it's soft, for about 5 minutes, stirring frequently. Add the garlic and cook for 1 minute. Turn off the Instant Pot.

Add the chicken broth and stir to scrape up all the browned bits from the bottom of the pot. Add the salsa verde to the pot, then add the chicken.

Close and lock the lid of the Instant Pot. Press "Manual" and immediately adjust the timer to 15 minutes. Check that the cooking pressure is on "High" and that the release valve is set to "Sealing."

When the time is up, open the Instant Pot using "Quick Pressure Release." Remove the chicken, cut it into bite-sized pieces, then return it to the pot. Taste, then season with salt and pepper. Pour the mixture in a baking dish and sprinkle with the cheeses. Cover the dish and allow the cheese to melt for a couple of minutes, or pop it under the broiler. Sprinkle with the chopped cilantro and serve.

# CAJUN CHICKEN ALFREDO

This might just be my favorite recipe in this whole book! It's so flavorful and creamy—such an indulgence. You can omit the Cajun seasoning if you prefer "regular" chicken alfredo. Serve this easy entrée with a side salad and crusty bread.

**YIELD: 4 TO 6 SERVINGS**

½ cup (114 g) unsalted butter

5 cloves garlic, minced

1 tbsp (8 g) plus 1 tsp Cajun seasoning

3 cups (708 ml) chicken broth

16 oz (454 g) fettucine, broken to fit the pot

2 lb (900 g) frozen chicken tenders

2 cups (472 ml) heavy cream

2 tsp (6 g) coarse salt

1 tsp freshly ground black pepper

2 cups (360 g) grated Parmesan cheese

¼ cup (10 g) chopped parsley

Press "Saute" to preheat your Instant Pot. When the word "Hot" appears on the display, add the butter. When the butter is almost completely melted, add the garlic and Cajun seasoning and cook for 1 minute. Turn off the Instant Pot and remove the inner pot to stop the cooking process. Add the broth, stirring well to scrape up any browned bits from the bottom. Add the fettucine, then the chicken. Close and lock the lid of the Instant Pot. Press "Manual" and immediately adjust the timer to 5 minutes. Check that the cooking pressure is on "High" and that the release valve is set to "Sealing."

When the time is up, open the Instant Pot using "Quick Pressure Release." Press "Cancel," then immediately press "Saute." Add the cream, salt, pepper and Parmesan cheese and bring to a simmer to thicken, stirring constantly (just a minute or two). Sprinkle with the parsley.

# SUN-DRIED TOMATO AND BASIL CHICKEN

This easy chicken dish is so flavorful and tastes like an upscale dish you cooked for hours, despite the few ingredients. The butter helps turn it into a creamy sauce that's perfect with a crusty bread to soak it all up. Don't skip the sun-dried tomatoes as they really bring the flavors in this recipe together.

**YIELD: 4 TO 6 SERVINGS**

¼ cup (57 g) unsalted butter, divided

¼ medium onion, chopped

5 cloves garlic, minced

½ cup (118 ml) low-sodium chicken broth

½ cup (118 ml) dry white wine

¼ cup (59 ml) fresh lemon juice

2 lb (900 g) frozen chicken tenders

1 cup (152 g) crumbled feta cheese

½ cup (55 g) sun-dried tomatoes in oil, drained and chopped

¼ cup (10 g) chopped fresh basil

½ tsp each coarse salt and freshly ground black pepper, plus more to taste

Press "Saute" to preheat your Instant Pot. When the word "Hot" appears on the display, add the butter. When the butter is melted, add the onion and cook until it's soft, for about 5 minutes, stirring frequently. Add the garlic and cook for 1 minute, stirring constantly. Turn off the Instant Pot.

Add the broth, wine and lemon juice to the pot, stirring well to scrape up any browned bits from the bottom. Add the chicken. Close and lock the lid of the Instant Pot. Press "Manual" and immediately adjust the timer to 8 minutes. Check that the cooking pressure is on "High" and that the release valve is set to "Sealing."

When the time is up, open the Instant Pot using "Quick Pressure Release." Add the feta, sun-dried tomatoes and basil to the pot. Season with salt and pepper.

# 40-CLOVE GARLIC CHICKEN AND POTATOES

If you love garlic, this is the recipe for you! The Instant Pot practically melts the garlic into the sauce and creates wonderful flavor. Don't be afraid of the amount of garlic called for—it mellows much like roasted garlic. This is a great recipe to enlist the help of the kids; they can peel the garlic cloves while you get the rest of the ingredients together.

**YIELD: 4 TO 6 SERVINGS**

¼ cup (57 g) unsalted butter

40 cloves garlic, peeled

¼ cup (59 ml) dry white wine

¾ cup (177 ml) low-sodium chicken broth

8 frozen bone-in chicken thighs

4 large thyme sprigs

1 lb (454 g) baby potatoes, cut in half if large

1 tbsp (8 g) cornstarch

1 tbsp (15 ml) cold water

1 tsp coarse salt

Freshly ground black pepper

Press "Saute" to preheat your Instant Pot. When the word "Hot" appears on the display, add the butter. When the butter is melted, add the garlic cloves and cook for a few minutes until the butter and cloves are just starting to brown. Remove the insert from the Instant Pot to stop the cooking process and press "Cancel" on the Instant Pot to turn it off.

Add the wine and broth, stirring well to scrape up any browned bits from the bottom. Add the chicken, thyme sprigs and potatoes to the pot. Return the insert to the Instant Pot. Press "Manual" and immediately adjust the timer to 30 minutes. Check that the cooking pressure is on "High" and that the release valve is set to "Sealing."

When the time is up, open the Instant Pot using "Quick Pressure Release." Remove the chicken to a broiler pan and broil for approximately 5 minutes, until the skin has crisped and browned.

Meanwhile, separate the fat from the liquid in the pot, discarding the fat and returning the remaining liquid to the pot. Press "Saute" on the Instant Pot.

Mix together the cornstarch and water. When the liquid is at a boil, add the cornstarch mixture to the liquid and stir for about a minute or until the sauce has thickened. Season with salt and pepper. Serve the sauce with the chicken.

# CRISPY ASIAN DRUMSTICKS

These simple chicken drumsticks will become a family favorite! The Instant Pot makes the chicken incredibly tender, and a quick turn under the broiler will crisp up the skin. You can make the sauce as spicy (or not) as you like. Sometimes I'll double the sauce, put it in two small dishes and season them at two heat levels so everyone is happy.

**YIELD: 4 TO 6 SERVINGS**

1 cup (236 ml) chicken broth or water

3 lb (1.3 kg) frozen chicken drumsticks

2 cloves garlic, minced

¼ tsp cayenne pepper

2 tbsp (30 ml) hoisin sauce

2 tbsp (30 ml) soy sauce

¼ cup (60 ml) honey

2 tsp (10 ml) sesame oil

2 tsp (10 ml) Sriracha (or to taste)

2 tbsp (18 g) sesame seeds

¼ cup (10 g) chopped green onions

Add the chicken broth or water to the pot, then add the drumsticks.

Close and lock the lid of the Instant Pot. Press "Manual" and immediately adjust the timer to 25 minutes. Check that the cooking pressure is on "High" and that the release valve is set to "Sealing."

While the chicken is cooking, mix together the garlic, cayenne, hoisin and soy sauces, honey, sesame oil and Sriracha. Set it aside.

When the time is up, open the Instant Pot using "Quick Pressure Release." Remove the chicken from the pot and place it on a broiler pan. Broil until the chicken is browned and crispy, for about 5 minutes or so per side. Add a spoonful of sauce on each piece of chicken, then sprinkle the chicken with the sesame seeds and chopped green onions. Serve with extra sauce at the table.

# GARLIC BUTTER CHICKEN, POTATOES AND ASPARAGUS

The method of adding potatoes, then broiling it together with some asparagus, can be used in many of the recipes in this book. It's a wonderful way to utilize your Instant Pot and your broiler together to make a delicious, healthy and quick meal. Not to mention the garlic and lemon flavors really make this dish pop.

**YIELD: 4 SERVINGS**

¼ cup (59 ml) fresh lemon juice

¼ cup (59 ml) low-sodium chicken broth

4 cloves garlic, minced

1 tsp dried oregano

1 lb (454 g) baby potatoes, about 1 inch (2.5 cm) across (cut in half to size)

4 frozen bone-in chicken thighs

½ lb (227 g) thin asparagus stalks, ends trimmed

¼ cup (57 g) unsalted butter, melted

1 tsp coarse salt

Freshly ground black pepper

Add the lemon juice, chicken broth, garlic and oregano to the pot. Add the potatoes to the pot, directly into the liquid, then place the chicken on top.

Close and lock the lid of the Instant Pot. Press "Manual" and immediately adjust the timer to 30 minutes. Check that the cooking pressure is on "High" and that the release valve is set to "Sealing."

When the time is up, open the Instant Pot using "Quick Pressure Release." Remove the chicken and potatoes and place them on a large sheet pan along with the asparagus, discarding the liquid in the pot. Brush the butter onto the chicken, potatoes and asparagus, then sprinkle with the salt and pepper.

Broil until the chicken skin is browned and crispy and the asparagus is crisp-tender, for about 5 minutes.

# PESTO CHICKEN AND RICE

Prepared pesto combined with frozen chicken and vegetables make this complete meal a breeze! Although any vegetable mix will work in this dish, I prefer peas, carrots and onions, which taste wonderful with the pesto.

## YIELD: 4 TO 6 SERVINGS

2 tbsp (28 g) unsalted butter

¼ medium onion, chopped

2 cloves garlic, minced

1 cup (185 g) dry brown rice, rinsed

1 cup (236 ml) low-sodium chicken broth

1 lb (454 g) frozen boneless, skinless chicken thighs

1 (16-oz [454-g]) bag frozen mixed vegetables

½ cup (113 g) prepared basil pesto

Coarse salt and freshly ground black pepper

Press "Saute" to preheat your Instant Pot. When the word "Hot" appears on the display, add the butter. When the butter is melted, add the onion and cook until it's soft, for about 5 minutes, stirring frequently. Add the garlic and cook for 1 minute. Remove the insert to stop the cooking process and press "Cancel" on the Instant Pot to turn it off.

Add the rice and broth to the pot, stirring well to scrape up any browned bits from the bottom. Add the chicken and vegetables and return the insert to the pot. Press "Manual" and immediately adjust the timer to 22 minutes. Check that the cooking pressure is on "High" and that the release valve is set to "Sealing."

When the time is up, open the Instant Pot using "Quick Pressure Release." Remove the chicken to a cutting board, cut it into bite-sized pieces and return it to the pot. Gently stir in the pesto. Season with salt and pepper.

# CREAMY ARTICHOKE CHICKEN

The Instant Pot takes your frozen chicken and makes it tender and juicy with so little effort! Serve this rich chicken dish with a side of rice and roasted asparagus, which can be made while the chicken is cooking. Drizzle some of the sauce over the rice and asparagus or serve it all together in bowls if you like.

YIELD: 4 TO 6 SERVINGS

2 tsp (10 ml) extra-virgin olive oil

1 clove garlic, minced

¼ cup (59 ml) low-sodium chicken broth

¼ cup (59 ml) dry white wine

Juice and zest from 1 lemon

8 frozen bone-in chicken thighs

½ cup (118 ml) heavy cream

1 (14-oz [396-g]) can quartered artichoke hearts, drained

½ cup (50 g) grated Parmesan cheese

¼ cup (38 g) crumbled feta cheese

Press "Saute" to preheat your Instant Pot. When the word "Hot" appears on the display, add the olive oil. When the oil is shimmering, add the garlic and cook for about a minute. Turn off the Instant Pot.

Add the chicken broth, wine, lemon juice and zest, then stir to scrape up all the browned bits from the bottom of the pot. Add the chicken to the pot, directly in the liquid.

Close and lock the lid of the Instant Pot. Press "Manual" and immediately adjust the timer to 30 minutes. Check that the cooking pressure is on "High" and that the release valve is set to "Sealing."

When the time is up, open the Instant Pot using "Quick Pressure Release." Remove the chicken and place it in a 13 x 9–inch (33 x 23–cm) baking dish. Remove the fat from the liquid in the pot and discard it, then stir in the cream, artichoke hearts and Parmesan cheese. Pour the sauce around the chicken in the baking dish.

Broil until the chicken skin is browned and crispy, for about 5 minutes. Top with the feta cheese and serve.

# TERIYAKI AND PINEAPPLE CHICKEN

The flavors of teriyaki and pineapple go so well together, much like frozen chicken and the Instant Pot! Brushing a little of the sauce onto the pineapple helps it to caramelize for even more flavor. Serve this with plenty of rice to soak up the delicious sauce.

## YIELD: 4 TO 6 SERVINGS

1 cup (236 ml) water

¼ cup (59 ml) soy sauce

½ tsp garlic powder

1 tsp ground ginger

¼ cup (55 g) brown sugar, packed

2 tbsp (30 ml) honey

8 frozen bone-in, skin-on chicken thighs

8 slices fresh pineapple

2 tbsp (16 g) cornstarch

2 tbsp (30 ml) cold water

2 tbsp (18 g) sesame seeds

¼ cup (10 g) chopped green onion

Mix together the water, soy sauce, garlic powder, ginger, brown sugar and honey, then add it to the pot. Place the chicken directly in the liquid.

Close and lock the lid of the Instant Pot. Press "Manual" and immediately adjust the timer to 30 minutes. Check that the cooking pressure is on "High" and that the release valve is set to "Sealing."

When the time is up, open the Instant Pot using "Quick Pressure Release." Remove the chicken and place it on a large sheet pan with the pineapple slices. Separate the fat from the liquid in the pot and discard, then return the liquid to the pot. Press "Cancel," then "Saute" and bring the liquid in the pot to a boil.

Mix the cornstarch and cold water together, then stir it into the hot liquid. Stir for about a minute to thicken the sauce.

Brush a small amount of sauce onto the chicken thighs and pineapple. Broil for about 5 minutes, until the chicken skin is browned and crispy. Sprinkle the chicken with the sesame seeds and green onions.

# CHICKEN WITH CREAMY MUSHROOM GARLIC SAUCE

This versatile recipe can also be made using beef or pork, if you prefer. Just skip the browning step at the end, otherwise all ingredients and amounts remain the same. In any case, your family will love the creamy garlic sauce that is perfect over rice or mashed potatoes.

**YIELD: 4 TO 6 SERVINGS**

2 tbsp (28 g) unsalted butter

1 lb (454 g) sliced mushrooms

1 medium onion, chopped

4 cloves garlic, minced

1 cup (236 ml) low-sodium chicken broth

8 frozen bone-in, skin-on chicken thighs

½ cup (118 ml) heavy cream

2 tbsp (16 g) cornstarch

2 tbsp (30 ml) cold water

¼ cup (25 g) grated Parmesan cheese

½ tsp each coarse salt and freshly ground black pepper, plus more to taste

2 tbsp (5 g) chopped fresh parsley

Press "Saute" to preheat your Instant Pot. When the word "Hot" appears on the display, add the butter. When the butter has almost melted, add the mushrooms and the onion and cook until the mushrooms are lightly browned, about 8 minutes. Add the garlic and cook for about a minute. Turn off the Instant Pot.

Add the chicken broth, then stir to scrape up all the browned bits from the bottom of the pot. Add the chicken to the pot, directly into the liquid.

Close and lock the lid of the Instant Pot. Press "Manual" and immediately adjust the timer to 30 minutes. Check that the cooking pressure is on "High" and that the release valve is set to "Sealing."

When the time is up, open the Instant Pot using "Quick Pressure Release." Remove the chicken and set it aside on a broiler pan. Remove the fat from the liquid in the pot and discard it, then stir in the cream. Press "Cancel," then "Saute."

Mix the cornstarch and cold water together. When the liquid in the pot is boiling, add the cornstarch "slurry" and stir for at least a minute, or until the sauce has thickened. Stir in the Parmesan cheese, salt, pepper and parsley. Turn off the Instant Pot.

Broil the chicken until the skin is browned and crispy, for about 5 minutes. Top with the sauce and serve.

# CHICKEN OSSO BUCO

Osso buco is one of those dishes that traditionally takes hours to braise. Not so with your Instant Pot! Your frozen chicken will be so fall-off-the-bone tender you'll be amazed it cooked that quickly yet still has the depth of flavor you love.

**YIELD: 4 TO 6 SERVINGS**

1 tbsp (15 ml) extra-virgin olive oil

1 medium onion, chopped

2 carrots, chopped

1 celery stalk, chopped

3 cloves garlic, minced

½ tsp rosemary

½ tsp thyme

1 tbsp (14 g) tomato paste

1 cup (240 ml) dry white wine

1 cup (236 ml) low-sodium chicken broth

1 (14.5-oz [411-g]) can fire-roasted diced tomatoes, with liquid

8 frozen, bone-in, skin-on chicken thighs

2 tbsp (16 g) cornstarch

2 tbsp (30 ml) cold water

2 tbsp (5 g) chopped fresh parsley

Crusty bread, for serving

Press "Saute" to preheat your Instant Pot. When the word "Hot" appears on the display, add the oil. When the oil is shimmering, add the onion, carrots and celery and cook until the onion is soft, for about 5 minutes. Add the garlic, rosemary and thyme and cook for about a minute. Add the tomato paste and cook for 1 minute. Add the wine and cook until it's reduced by two-thirds, about 6 minutes, taking care to scrape up any browned bits from the bottom of the pot. Turn off the Instant Pot.

Add the chicken broth and tomatoes, then add the chicken.

Close and lock the lid of the Instant Pot. Press "Manual" and immediately adjust the timer to 30 minutes. Check that the cooking pressure is on "High" and that the release valve is set to "Sealing."

When the time is up, open the Instant Pot using "Quick Pressure Release." Remove the chicken and set it aside on a broiler pan. Press "Cancel," then "Saute." Mix together the cornstarch and cold water. When the liquid in the pot is boiling, add the cornstarch "slurry" and cook for at least a minute or until the sauce has thickened. Turn off the Instant Pot and stir in the parsley.

Broil the chicken until the skin is browned and crispy, for about 5 minutes. Serve the chicken and sauce in large bowls with a side of crusty bread.

# MOROCCAN CHICKEN AND POTATOES

I traveled through Morocco a few years ago, taking cooking classes and learning about the culture. This is one of my favorite spice combinations I learned while there, and I make sure to keep these spices on hand so I can make it on busy weeknights without having to run to the store. I added potatoes for a more complete meal, but you can omit them and serve this delicious dish over rice if you prefer.

**YIELD: 4 TO 6 SERVINGS**

1 tsp paprika

½ tsp ground ginger

½ tsp cinnamon

½ tsp cumin

½ tsp coarse salt

¼ tsp freshly ground black pepper

1 cup (236 ml) chicken broth

8 frozen bone-in, skin-on chicken thighs

1 lb (454 g) baby red potatoes

¼ cup (57 g) unsalted butter, melted

Mix together the paprika, ginger, cinnamon, cumin, salt and black pepper and set it aside.

Add the chicken broth to the pot, then add the chicken and potatoes. Close and lock the lid of the Instant Pot. Press "Manual" and immediately adjust the timer to 30 minutes. Check that the cooking pressure is on "High" and that the release valve is set to "Sealing."

When the time is up, open the Instant Pot using "Quick Pressure Release." Remove the chicken and place it on a broiler pan. Turn off the Instant Pot.

Broil the chicken until the skin is browned and crispy, for about 5 minutes or so. Place the chicken and potatoes on a serving dish. Mix together the spice mixture and melted butter, then brush it on the chicken and potatoes and serve.

# GREEK CHICKEN BOWLS WITH TZATZIKI

This is one of my favorite healthy lunches. It's easy to double or triple the recipe to make enough to prep the whole family's lunches for the week. It will take your Instant Pot slightly longer to come to pressure, but you don't need to increase the cooking time.

**YIELD: 4 SERVINGS**

### FOR THE CHICKEN

2 lb (900 g) frozen boneless, skinless chicken breasts

½ cup (118 ml) chicken broth

⅓ cup (78 ml) fresh lemon juice

4 cloves garlic, minced

2 tbsp (6 g) dried oregano

1 tsp dried rosemary

1 tsp dried thyme

### FOR THE TZATZIKI

2 cups (400 g) plain Greek yogurt

3 cloves garlic, finely minced or pressed

Juice of ½ lemon

¼ cup (2 g) chopped fresh dill

½ tsp coarse salt

¼ tsp freshly ground black pepper

### FOR SERVING

2 cups (300 g) cherry tomatoes, halved

2 cucumbers, chopped

Place the chicken breasts, broth, lemon juice, garlic, oregano, rosemary and thyme into the Instant Pot.

Close and lock the lid of the Instant Pot. Press "Manual" and immediately adjust the timer to 10 minutes. Check that the cooking pressure is on "High" and that the release valve is set to "Sealing."

Meanwhile, mix together the ingredients for the tzatziki sauce in a bowl and set it aside.

When the time is up, open the Instant Pot using "Quick Pressure Release." Remove the chicken to a cutting board and cut it into bite-sized pieces.

Serve the chicken with the halved cherry tomatoes, sliced cucumbers and the tzatziki sauce for a delicious, healthy lunch or light dinner.

# LIGHTNING FAST BEEF AND PORK ENTRÉES

Beef and pork are two meats I've always dreaded having to thaw since they can take such a long time. I've never been able to quite manage it unless I think about it the night before and put a small, frozen roast in the refrigerator. Now I freeze my large roasts in smaller portions so I can toss them into my Instant Pot straight from the freezer. The recipes in this chapter have some delicious flavor twists your family will love!

**MY THREE FAVORITES**
Beef and Blue Cheese Stroganoff (page 53)
Meatballs in Tomato-Chipotle Sauce (page 65)
Beef and Barley Pot Pie with Buttery Parmesan Biscuits (page 73)

# COWBOY BEEF AND SAUSAGE STEW

This is called "cowboy" stew because it's hearty and has loads of flavorful, tender meat in it. I added some vegetables too, as well as potatoes, for a well-rounded meal any cowboy would be glad to enjoy. The bacon, red wine and sausage turn it into a meal you'll want to enjoy again and again.

## YIELD: 8 SERVINGS

6 slices bacon, sliced crosswise into 1-inch (2.5-cm) pieces

2 lb (900 g) cubed frozen beef stew meat

1 large onion, chopped

2 cloves garlic, minced

1 cup (236 ml) pinot noir wine

1 lb (454 g) baby potatoes, cut into bite-sized pieces

4 cups (946 ml) low-sodium beef broth

2 (14.5-oz [411-g]) cans fire-roasted diced tomatoes, with liquid

1 (10-oz [284-g]) package frozen mixed vegetables

1 lb (454 g) fresh or frozen andouille sausage links

1 bay leaf

2 thyme sprigs

Coarse salt and freshly ground black pepper

Press "Saute" to preheat your Instant Pot. When the word "Hot" appears on the display, add the bacon and cook until it's browned and crisp; then remove it with a slotted spoon and set it aside. Add the cubed beef to the bacon drippings. Cook until it's browned, in batches if necessary, then set it aside.

Add the onion and cook until it's soft, for about 5 minutes, stirring frequently. Add the garlic and cook for 1 minute. Add the wine and cook until it's reduced by half, for about 4 to 5 minutes, taking care to scrape up all the browned bits on the bottom of the pot. Turn off the Instant Pot.

Add the potatoes, beef broth, tomatoes, frozen vegetables, sausage, bay leaf and thyme sprigs to the pot. Close and lock the lid of the Instant Pot. Press "Manual" and immediately adjust the timer to 30 minutes. Check that the cooking pressure is on "High" and that the release valve is set to "Sealing."

When the time is up, allow the pressure to release naturally for 10 minutes, then open the Instant Pot using "Quick Pressure Release." Remove the sausage links and cut them into bite-sized pieces, then return them to the pot. Remove the bay leaf and discard it, then taste and season with salt and pepper.

# BEEF AND BLUE CHEESE STROGANOFF

Stroganoff was a dish my mom made often when I was growing up. This version has the twist of creamy blue cheese and is easy enough for a weeknight, yet has flavors sophisticated enough to serve when company is over. Be sure to add lots of freshly ground black pepper if you like.

## YIELD: 4 TO 6 SERVINGS

2 tsp (10 ml) extra-virgin olive oil

1 lb (454 g) frozen sirloin

1 lb (454 g) sliced mushrooms

½ medium onion, chopped

2 cloves garlic, minced

2 tbsp (28 g) unsalted butter

2 tbsp (15 g) flour

2 cups (472 ml) reduced sodium beef broth

½ cup (115 g) sour cream

4 oz (113 g) crumbled blue cheese

2 tsp (10 ml) Dijon mustard

2 tbsp (6 g) chopped chives

Coarse salt and freshly ground black pepper

Cooked egg noodles, rice or mashed potatoes, for serving

Press "Saute" to preheat your Instant Pot. When the word "Hot" appears on the display, add the olive oil. When the oil is shimmering, add the sirloin. Brown it well on both sides, 3 to 4 minutes per side, then set it aside.

Add the mushrooms and onion, and cook until the mushrooms have released their liquid and it has evaporated, for about 5 minutes. Add the garlic and cook for 1 minute. Add the butter; once melted, sprinkle the flour into the pot. Stir continually for 1 minute. Turn off the Instant Pot.

Add the reserved sirloin and the beef broth, stirring well to scrape up any browned bits from the bottom. Close and lock the lid of the Instant Pot. Press "Manual" and immediately adjust the timer to 20 minutes. Check that the cooking pressure is on "High" and that the release valve is set to "Sealing."

When the time is up, allow the pressure to release naturally for 10 minutes, then open the Instant Pot using "Quick Pressure Release." Remove the sirloin and shred it with two forks. Press "Cancel," then "Saute" on the Instant Pot. Add the sour cream, blue cheese and Dijon, stirring until the sauce is smooth and the cheese is melted. Add the sirloin back to the pot along with the chives. Taste, then season with salt and pepper.

Serve over cooked egg noodles, rice or mashed potatoes.

# PULLED PORK CHILI

I love using a pork rib roast in this recipe, but feel free to substitute a loin if that's what you have on hand. The pork will practically fall apart on its own! This chili is one of my favorites since it starts with dried beans and almost all pantry ingredients.

## YIELD: 6 SERVINGS

2 tsp (10 ml) extra-virgin olive oil

1 large onion, chopped

3 cloves garlic, minced

1 tbsp (8 g) chili powder

1 tsp ground cumin

1 tbsp (16 g) tomato paste

1 cup (236 ml) chicken broth

1 (14.5-oz [411-g]) can fire-roasted diced tomatoes, with liquid

1 tbsp (18 g) adobo sauce (from a can of chipotle chiles)

1 cup (194 g) dried black beans

2 lb (900 g) frozen pork rib roast

Coarse salt and freshly ground black pepper

½ cup (20 g) chopped cilantro

Press "Saute" to preheat your Instant Pot. When the word "Hot" appears on the display, add the olive oil. When the oil is shimmering, add the onion and cook until it is soft, for about 5 minutes, stirring frequently. Add the garlic, chili powder and cumin and cook for 1 more minute. Add the tomato paste and cook for another minute. Turn off the Instant Pot.

Add the chicken broth and stir to scrape up all the browned bits from the bottom of the pot. Stir in the tomatoes, adobo sauce and black beans. Nestle the rib roast into the liquid.

Close and lock the lid of the Instant Pot. Press "Manual" and immediately adjust the timer to 60 minutes. Check that the cooking pressure is on "High" and that the release valve is set to "Sealing."

When the time is up, allow the pressure to release naturally before opening the pot. Remove the pork roast, shred it with two forks, then return it to the pot. Taste, then season with salt and pepper. Sprinkle with the chopped cilantro and serve.

# PORK VERDE CHILI

This easy chili is filled with flavor and you'll love how the pork will simply melt in your mouth. The extra step of blackening the fresh tomatillos is worth it, trust me! This chili freezes well so you can save half for a quick weeknight meal. Be sure to cut your meat before freezing it (see the tips section on page 7).

YIELD: 8 SERVINGS

1½ lb (681 g) fresh tomatillos, halved

3 poblano chile peppers

2 jalapeño peppers

4 tsp (20 ml) extra-virgin olive oil, divided

½ cup (20 g) chopped cilantro

2 large onions, chopped

5 cloves garlic, minced

1 tbsp (3 g) dried oregano

1 tsp cumin

2 cups (472 ml) chicken broth

4 lb (1.8 kg) frozen pork shoulder, cut into 4 pieces

Coarse salt and freshly ground black pepper

Cooked rice, for serving

Place the tomatillos, poblanos and jalapeños onto a sheet pan and toss with 2 teaspoons (10 ml) of olive oil. Place them under the broiler and blacken all sides. Remove them from the oven and take the stem and seeds from the poblanos and jalapeños. Place them in a blender with the cilantro and puree until smooth.

Press "Saute" to preheat your Instant Pot. When the word "Hot" appears on the display, add the remaining 2 teaspoons (10 ml) of olive oil. When the oil is shimmering, add the onions. Cook until the onions are soft, for about 5 minutes, stirring frequently. Add the garlic, oregano and cumin and cook for 1 minute, stirring frequently. Turn off the Instant Pot.

Add the chicken broth, stirring well to scrape up any browned bits from the bottom. Place the pork pieces directly into the broth mixture. Pour the tomatillo mixture over the pork.

Close and lock the lid of the Instant Pot. Press "Manual" and immediately adjust the timer to 45 minutes. Check that the cooking pressure is on "High" and that the release valve is set to "Sealing."

When the time is up, open the Instant Pot using "Quick Pressure Release." Gently break the pork apart into bite-sized chunks using two forks. Serve with rice.

# BEEFY SPANISH RICE

This recipe is reminiscent of a rice dish my mom made often when I was growing up. I've added beef to mine to make it more of a main dish than a side, but you could leave it out if you prefer. The cooking time will remain the same, so make it a main or a side dish to suit your needs.

**YIELD: 4 TO 6 SERVINGS**

1 tbsp (15 ml) extra-virgin olive oil

1 lb (454 g) frozen sirloin

½ medium onion, chopped

2 cloves garlic, minced

1 tsp chipotle chile powder

½ tsp ground cumin

1 cup (185 g) long-grain white rice, rinsed

2 cups (472 ml) low-sodium beef broth

1 (16-oz [454-g]) jar red salsa

1 (15-oz [425-g]) can black beans, rinsed and drained

1 (14.5-oz [418-g]) can fire-roasted corn, drained

1 (14.5-oz [411-g]) can fire-roasted diced tomatoes, with liquid

Coarse salt and freshly ground black pepper

Press "Saute" to preheat your Instant Pot. When the word "Hot" appears on the display, add the olive oil. When the oil is shimmering, add the sirloin. Brown it well on both sides, 3 to 4 minutes per side, then set it aside.

Add the onion and cook until it's soft, for about 5 minutes. Add the garlic, chipotle powder and cumin and cook for 1 minute. Turn off the Instant Pot.

Add the rice, reserved sirloin and the beef broth, stirring well to scrape up any browned bits from the bottom. Add the salsa, black beans, corn and tomatoes. Close and lock the lid of the Instant Pot. Press "Manual" and immediately adjust the timer to 10 minutes. Check that the cooking pressure is on "High" and that the release valve is set to "Sealing."

When the time is up, open the Instant Pot using "Quick Pressure Release." Remove the sirloin and shred it with two forks, then return it to the pot and mix it in. Taste, then season with salt and pepper.

# PORK TENDERLOIN WITH APPLE CIDER SAUCE

This delicious apple cider sauce is perfect for a cold, fall evening. It's best with fresh apple cider, but if the bottled is all you can get, that will work too! The butter and cream make it a delightfully creamy sauce that goes perfectly with the tender pork loin.

**YIELD: 4 TO 6 SERVINGS**

2 lb (900 g) frozen pork loin

½ cup (118 ml) low-sodium chicken broth

2 cups (472 ml) apple cider (not juice)

2 thyme sprigs

2 tbsp (16 g) cornstarch

2 tbsp (30 ml) cold water

¼ cup (59 ml) heavy cream

2 tbsp (28 g) unsalted butter, cut into four pieces

1 tsp coarse salt

Freshly ground black pepper

Mashed potatoes, for serving

Place the pork, broth, cider and thyme sprigs in the pot. Close and lock the lid of the Instant Pot. Press "Manual" and immediately adjust the timer to 45 minutes. Check that the cooking pressure is on "High" and that the release valve is set to "Sealing."

When the time is up, allow the pressure to release naturally for 10 minutes, then open the Instant Pot using "Quick Pressure Release." Remove the pork from the pot and set it aside. Skim off the fat from the liquid in the pot and discard it. Press "Cancel," then immediately press "Saute." Boil until the liquid in the pot is reduced by half, for about 10 minutes.

Mix together the cornstarch and water. Pour the "slurry" into the boiling liquid in the pot and stir for at least 1 minute, or until the sauce is thickened. Stir in the cream and butter, stirring until smooth. Season with salt and pepper.

Slice the pork and serve it with sauce over mashed potatoes.

# PORK CHOPS WITH JALAPEÑO PEACH SAUCE

This jalapeño peach sauce is one of my dad's favorites. He and I both like spicy food, so I make this for him often. You could also use a chipotle pepper in place of the jalapeño—or in addition to, if you really like spice—to add a smoky bite.

**YIELD: 4 SERVINGS**

2 tsp (10 ml) extra-virgin olive oil

¼ cup (40 g) minced red onion

1 jalapeño pepper, minced

1 clove garlic, minced

¼ cup (59 ml) chicken broth

1 (12-oz [340-g]) bag frozen sliced peaches

¼ cup (59 ml) peach preserves

4 frozen, bone-in pork chops

¼ cup (10 g) chopped cilantro

Coarse salt and freshly ground black pepper

Press "Saute" to preheat your Instant Pot. When the word "Hot" appears on the display, add the olive oil. When the oil is shimmering, add the onion and jalapeño. Cook until the onion is soft, for about 5 minutes, stirring frequently. Add the garlic and cook for 1 minute. Turn off the Instant Pot.

Add the chicken broth, stirring well to scrape up any browned bits from the bottom.

Add the peaches, preserves and pork chops to the pot. Close and lock the lid of the Instant Pot. Press "Manual" and immediately adjust the timer to 10 minutes. Check that the cooking pressure is on "High" and that the release valve is set to "Sealing."

When the time is up, allow the pressure to release naturally for 10 minutes, then open the Instant Pot using "Quick Pressure Release." Stir in the cilantro. Taste the sauce, then season with salt and pepper.

# MEATBALLS IN TOMATO-CHIPOTLE SAUCE

These meatballs are one of my favorite recipes in this book. They are so simple, but this isn't your run-of-the-mill tomato sauce; the addition of cumin and chipotle creates a slightly smoky sauce that will have your family guessing what secret ingredients you've added. I like to serve them with traditional Mexican side dishes for a fun weeknight meal.

**YIELD: 4 TO 6 SERVINGS**

2 tsp (10 ml) extra-virgin olive oil

½ medium onion, chopped

2 cloves garlic, minced

1 tsp ground cumin

¼ cup (59 ml) chicken broth

2 lb (900 g) frozen meatballs

1 (28-oz [822-g]) can tomato puree

2 chipotle peppers (from a can of chipotles in adobo sauce)

Coarse salt and freshly ground black pepper

Press "Saute" to preheat your Instant Pot. When the word "Hot" appears on the display, add the olive oil. When the oil is shimmering, add the onion and cook until it's soft, for about 5 minutes, stirring frequently. Add the garlic and cumin and cook for 1 minute. Turn off the Instant Pot.

Add the chicken broth and stir to scrape up all the browned bits from the bottom of the pot. Add the meatballs, then pour the tomato puree over them (do not stir). Top with the chipotle peppers.

Close and lock the lid of the Instant Pot. Press "Manual" and immediately adjust the timer to 15 minutes. Check that the cooking pressure is on "High" and that the release valve is set to "Sealing."

When the time is up, allow the pressure to release naturally for 10 minutes, then open the pot using "Quick Pressure Release." Taste, then season with salt and pepper.

# HONEY MUSTARD–GLAZED PORK RIB ROAST

This roast has one of the longest cooking times in this book, but the rest of the steps are so simple that it actually takes less active time than some of the other recipes. In any case, it's a delicious family favorite, especially with the kids. Be sure to cut your roast before freezing it (see the tips section on page 7).

**YIELD: 4 TO 6 SERVINGS**

4 lb (1.8 kg) frozen pork rib roast, cut into 4 pieces

1 cup (236 ml) water or chicken broth

2 tbsp (16 g) brown sugar

2 tbsp (28 g) unsalted butter, melted

½ cup (118 ml) honey

3 tbsp (44 ml) Dijon mustard

Coarse salt and freshly ground black pepper

Add the roast and water or chicken broth to the pot. Close and lock the lid of the Instant Pot. Press "Manual" and immediately adjust the timer to 70 minutes. Check that the cooking pressure is on "High" and that the release valve is set to "Sealing."

Meanwhile, mix together the brown sugar, butter, honey, Dijon and salt and pepper to taste, then set it aside.

When the time is up, allow the pressure to release naturally for 10 minutes, then open the pot using "Quick Pressure Release." Place the roast on a broiler pan and brush it with the sauce. Broil for 5 minutes or so, until the sauce is bubbling and starting to caramelize.

# STEAK AND POTATOES WITH MUSHROOM GRAVY

Who doesn't love a dish where the steak and potatoes can all be tossed into the same pot? Especially when the steak starts from frozen and ends up so tender you can shred it with two forks! Toss some baby carrots into the pot along with the potatoes if you like.

**YIELD: 4 SERVINGS**

2 tsp (10 ml) extra-virgin olive oil

2 lb (900 g) frozen sirloin

1 lb (454 g) sliced mushrooms

1 medium onion, sliced

2 cloves garlic, minced

2 tbsp (28 g) unsalted butter

2 tbsp (15 g) flour

3 cups (708 ml) reduced-sodium beef broth

1 lb (454 g) baby red potatoes, about 1-inch (2.5-cm) thick (or cut to that size)

2 tsp (10 ml) Worcestershire sauce

Coarse salt and freshly ground black pepper

Press "Saute" to preheat your Instant Pot. When the word "Hot" appears on the display, add the olive oil. When the oil is shimmering, add the sirloin. Brown it well on both sides, 3 to 4 minutes per side, then set it aside.

Add the mushrooms and onion and cook until the mushrooms have released their liquid and it has evaporated, for about 5 minutes. Add the garlic and cook for 1 minute. Add the butter; once melted, sprinkle the flour into the pot. Stir continually for 1 minute. Turn off the Instant Pot.

Add the reserved sirloin and the beef broth, stirring well to scrape up any browned bits from the bottom. Add the potatoes. Close and lock the lid of the Instant Pot. Press "Manual" and immediately adjust the timer to 20 minutes. Check that the cooking pressure is on "High" and that the release valve is set to "Sealing."

When the time is up, allow the pressure to release naturally for 10 minutes, then open the Instant Pot using "Quick Pressure Release." Remove the sirloin and shred it with two forks. Press "Cancel," then "Saute" on the Instant Pot. Add the sirloin back to the pot. Add the Worcstershire sauce, taste, then season with salt and pepper.

# CHERRY-CHIPOTLE PORK CHOPS

One of the most popular recipes on my site is for a cherry chipotle salsa , which is what inspired me to make these delicious pork chops. The sweet cherries and smoky chipotle create a winning flavor combination you will love. They're so tender and flavorful, you'll be making them every week!

**YIELD: 4 SERVINGS**

2 tsp (10 ml) extra-virgin olive oil

1 large shallot, chopped

1 cup (155 g) frozen pitted cherries

½ cup (118 ml) chicken broth

1 chipotle pepper, minced (from a can of chipotles in adobo sauce)

4 frozen bone-in pork chops

½ cup (118 ml) cherry juice

1 tbsp (15 ml) fresh lemon juice

2 tbsp (28 g) unsalted butter

2 tbsp (5 g) chopped parsley

Coarse salt and freshly ground black pepper

Press "Saute" to preheat your Instant Pot. When the word "Hot" appears on the display, add the olive oil. When the oil is shimmering, add the shallot. Cook until the shallot is soft, for about 3 to 4 minutes, stirring frequently.

Add the cherries, chicken broth and chipotle pepper, stirring well to scrape up any browned bits from the bottom. Turn off the Instant Pot.

Add the pork chops to the pot. Close and lock the lid of the Instant Pot. Press "Manual" and immediately adjust the timer to 10 minutes. Check that the cooking pressure is on "High" and that the release valve is set to "Sealing."

When the time is up, allow the pressure to release naturally for 10 minutes, then open the Instant Pot using "Quick Pressure Release." Remove the chops from the pot and set them aside. Press "Cancel," then immediately press "Saute." Add the cherry juice and boil the liquid in the pot until it is reduced and thickened, about 5 minutes. Stir in the lemon juice, butter and parsley and season to taste with salt and pepper. Pour the sauce over the chops and serve.

# RIB-EYE STEAKS WITH RED-WINE PAN SAUCE

Who would have thought you can have an upscale dish like this come out of your Instant Pot, especially when you start with frozen meat? This is a great meal to have any night of the week, or save it for a special Valentine's dinner with your loved one.

**YIELD: 2 TO 3 SERVINGS**

¼ cup (57 g) unsalted butter, divided

1 medium shallot, chopped

¾ cup (177 ml) pinot noir wine

1 cup (236 ml) low-sodium beef broth

2 thyme sprigs

2 lb (900 g) frozen rib-eye steaks

2 tsp (10 ml) Dijon mustard

Coarse salt and freshly ground black pepper

Mashed potatoes, for serving

Press "Saute" to preheat your Instant Pot. When the word "Hot" appears on the display, add 2 tablespoons (29 g) of the butter. When the butter is almost melted, add the shallot and cook until it starts to soften, for about 5 minutes. Add the red wine and boil until it's reduced by half, about 5 minutes. Turn off the Instant Pot.

Add the beef broth, stirring well to scrape up any browned bits from the bottom. Add the thyme sprigs and steaks to the pot.

Close and lock the lid of the Instant Pot. Press "Manual" and immediately adjust the timer to 3 minutes. Check that the cooking pressure is on "High" and that the release valve is set to "Sealing."

When the time is up, open the Instant Pot using "Quick Pressure Release." Press "Cancel," then "Saute." Remove the steaks and set them aside. Boil the liquid until it's reduced by half, about 5 minutes. Stir in the Dijon and remaining 2 tablespoons (29 g) of butter, 1 tablespoon (14 g) at a time. Season with salt and pepper. Serve the steaks with the sauce and mashed potatoes.

*See photo on page 48.

# SUPER FAST SPAGHETTI AND MEATBALLS

This spaghetti and meatball dish is almost as simple as opening a jar of sauce and cooking the spaghetti in a pot of boiling water, but the flavor is so much better. I love that I can prepare the sauce and noodles in the same pot at the same time. Leave it to the Instant Pot to improve such a beloved dish!

## YIELD: 4 TO 6 SERVINGS

1 tbsp (15 ml) extra-virgin olive oil

1 medium onion, chopped

3 cloves garlic, minced

1 tbsp (8 g) Italian seasoning

1 tbsp (16 g) tomato paste

½ cup (118 ml) Malbec wine

3 cups (708 ml) low-sodium chicken broth

1 (15-oz [425-g]) can tomato sauce

2 (14.5-oz [411-g]) cans fire-roasted diced tomatoes, with liquid

1 lb (454 g) spaghetti pasta (broken to fit the pot)

1 lb (454 g) frozen Italian meatballs

¼ cup (25 g) grated Parmesan cheese

¼ cup (10 g) chopped fresh parsley

Press "Saute" to preheat your Instant Pot. When the word "Hot" appears on the display, add the oil. When the oil is shimmering, add the onion and cook until it's soft, for about 5 minutes. Add the garlic and Italian seasoning and cook for 1 minute. Add the tomato paste and cook 1 minute longer. Add the wine, stirring well to scrape up any browned bits from the bottom of the pot. Cook the wine until it's reduced by half, for about 5 minutes. Turn off the Instant Pot and remove the inner pot to stop the cooking process. Allow the contents to cool for 5 minutes, then place the inner pot back in the Instant Pot.

Add the broth, tomato sauce, tomatoes, pasta and meatballs to the pot, taking care to submerge the pasta completely (do not stir). Close and lock the lid of the Instant Pot. Press "Manual" and immediately adjust the timer to 6 minutes. Check that the cooking pressure is on "High" and that the release valve is set to "Sealing."

When the time is up, open the Instant Pot using "Quick Pressure Release." Gently stir, then top with the Parmesan cheese and parsley.

# BEEF AND BARLEY POT PIE WITH BUTTERY PARMESAN BISCUITS

The consistency of this pot pie is spot-on—not too thick, not too thin—which is something I'm particular about when it comes to pot pie. The biscuits are perfect as a topping, but so good you can make them all on their own for any number of meals. Be sure to cut the meat before freezing it (see the tips section on page 7) or shred it after cooking.

**YIELD: 6 TO 8 SERVINGS**

## FOR THE POT PIE

6 slices bacon, cut crosswise into 1-inch (2.5-cm) pieces

2 lb (900 g) frozen sirloin, cut into bite-sized cubes

1 medium onion, chopped

2 cloves garlic, minced

½ tsp dried thyme

1 tbsp (16 g) tomato paste

2 tbsp (15 g) flour

3 cups (708 ml) low-sodium beef broth

½ cup (100 g) barley

1 lb (454 g) red baby potatoes

3 cups (681 g) frozen mixed vegetables

2 tsp (10 ml) Worcestershire sauce

Coarse salt and freshly ground black pepper

## FOR THE BISCUITS

1 (16-oz [462-g]) can refrigerated biscuits (about 8 large biscuits)

3 tbsp (42 g) unsalted butter, melted

½ cup (50 g) grated Parmesan cheese

Press "Saute" to preheat your Instant Pot. When the word "Hot" appears on the display, add the bacon and cook until it's browned and crisp, about 5 minutes, then remove it with a slotted spoon and set it aside. Add the cubed sirloin to the bacon drippings. Cook until it's browned, about 5 minutes, in batches if necessary, then set it aside.

Add the onion and cook until it's soft, for about 5 minutes, stirring frequently. Add the garlic and thyme and cook for 1 minute. Add the tomato paste and cook another minute. Add the flour and cook for 1 more minute, stirring constantly. Remove the insert from the Instant Pot to stop the cooking process and press "Cancel" on the Instant Pot to turn it off.

Add the beef broth, stirring to scrape up anything stuck to the bottom. Add the barley, potatoes, vegetables and reserved sirloin to the pot then return the pot to the base. Close and lock the lid of the Instant Pot. Press "Manual" and immediately adjust the timer to 30 minutes. Check that the cooking pressure is on "High" and that the release valve is set to "Sealing."

Meanwhile, make the biscuits by brushing the top of each biscuit with butter, sprinkling it with Parmesan cheese and baking according to the package directions.

When the time is up, allow the pressure to release naturally for 10 minutes, then open the Instant Pot using "Quick Pressure Release." Add the sirloin and bacon back to pot, add the Worcestershire sauce, then taste and season with salt and pepper. Top each bowl with a Buttery Parmesan Biscuit.

# BEEF WITH BROCCOLI

Who needs takeout when your Instant Pot makes such quick work of it? Not to mention it tastes better, is always piping hot and you know exactly what ingredients went into it. It's so much easier than ordering takeout, and the flavors are better too!

**YIELD: 4 SERVINGS**

2 lb (900 g) frozen boneless rib-eye steaks

Coarse salt and freshly ground black pepper

2 tsp (10 ml) extra-virgin olive oil

1 large onion, sliced

6 cloves garlic, minced

1 cup (236 ml) low-sodium beef broth

½ cup (118 ml) low-sodium soy sauce

1 tsp ground ginger

2 tbsp (28 g) brown sugar, packed

2 tbsp (16 g) cornstarch

2 tbsp (30 ml) cold water

1 (12-oz [340-g]) bag frozen broccoli (or fresh, if preferred)

Cooked rice, for serving

Remove the steaks from the freezer and allow them to thaw for 30 minutes. Slice the steaks against the grain very thinly. (Alternatively, if using fresh steaks, freeze them for 30 to 60 minutes, then slice.) Season the steaks with salt and pepper.

Press "Saute" to preheat your Instant Pot. When the word "Hot" appears on the display, add the olive oil. When the oil is shimmering, add the onion and cook until the onion is starting to soften, for about 5 minutes. Add the garlic and cook for 1 minute. Turn off the Instant Pot.

Add the beef broth, stirring well to scrape up any browned bits from the bottom. Add the soy sauce, ginger and brown sugar. Add the sliced steak to the pot. Close and lock the lid of the Instant Pot. Press "Manual" and immediately adjust the timer to 15 minutes. Check that the cooking pressure is on "High" and that the release valve is set to "Sealing."

When the time is up, open the Instant Pot using "Quick Pressure Release." Press "Cancel," then "Saute."

Mix together the cornstarch and water. When the liquid in the pot is boiling, pour the cornstarch "slurry" into the pot and stir for at least 1 minute, or until the sauce is thickened (it will thicken more as it cools).

Prepare the broccoli according to the package directions. Toss the broccoli with the sauce and beef. Serve over rice.

# CREAMY RANCH PORK CHOPS

This dish reminds me of my childhood. My mom's recipe includes a can of cream of chicken soup, but I use cream cheese and it's just as delicious (especially if you're a cream cheese lover like me)! I keep packets of dry ranch dressing mix on hand so I can make this at a moment's notice.

## YIELD: 4 TO 6 SERVINGS

1 tbsp (15 ml) extra-virgin olive oil

3 lb (1.4 kg) frozen bone-in pork chops

1 cup (236 ml) low-sodium chicken broth

¼ cup (57 g) unsalted butter

1 (1-oz [28-g]) packet ranch dressing mix

4 oz (113 g) cream cheese, softened

2 tbsp (5 g) chopped fresh parsley

Press "Saute" to preheat your Instant Pot. When the word "Hot" appears on the display, add the olive oil. When the oil is shimmering, add the pork chops and brown each side, 3 to 4 minutes per side, in batches if necessary. Add the chicken broth, stirring well to scrape up any browned bits from the bottom. Turn off the Instant Pot.

Add the butter and ranch dressing mix. Close and lock the lid of the Instant Pot. Press "Manual" and immediately adjust the timer to 10 minutes. Check that the cooking pressure is on "High" and that the release valve is set to "Sealing."

When the time is up, open the Instant Pot using "Quick Pressure Release." Remove the pork chops from the pot and set them aside. Press "Cancel," then immediately press "Saute." Add the cream cheese and stir until it's melted. Serve the sauce over the pork chops and sprinkle with the parsley.

# MONGOLIAN BEEF

Here's another takeout winner! The savory soy sauce and ginger combined with the slight spiciness from the crushed red pepper flakes will make you think you're seated at your favorite Chinese restaurant. Make a side of rice to soak up the extra sauce.

**YIELD: 4 SERVINGS**

1 lb (454 g) frozen flank steak

1 tbsp (15 ml) extra-virgin olive oil

5 cloves garlic, minced

1 cup (236 ml) water

½ cup (118 ml) soy sauce

1 tsp ground ginger

1 tsp sesame oil

1 tsp crushed red pepper flakes

½ cup (110 g) brown sugar, lightly packed

2 tbsp (16 g) cornstarch

2 tbsp (30 ml) cold water

4 green onions, chopped

1 tbsp (9 g) sesame seeds

Cooked rice, for serving

Remove the steak from the freezer and allow it to sit at room temperature for 30 to 45 minutes. Thinly slice the meat against the grain.

Press "Saute" to preheat your Instant Pot. When the word "Hot" appears on the display, add the olive oil. When the oil is shimmering, add the steak and cook until it's browned, for about 3 to 4 minutes. Add the garlic and cook for 1 minute.

Add the water to the pot, stirring well to scrape up any browned bits from the bottom. Turn off the Instant Pot.

Add the soy sauce, ginger, sesame oil, pepper flakes and brown sugar to the pot. Close and lock the lid of the Instant Pot. Press "Manual" and immediately adjust the timer to 10 minutes. Check that the cooking pressure is on "High" and that the release valve is set to "Sealing."

When the time is up, allow the pressure to release naturally for 5 minutes, then open it using "Quick Pressure Release." Press "Cancel," then press "Saute."

Mix together the cornstarch and water. When the liquid in the pot is boiling, add the cornstarch "slurry" and stir for at least 1 minute until the sauce is thickened.

Sprinkle with the green onions and sesame seeds and serve over rice.

# PARMESAN SOUR CREAM PORK CHOPS

These pork chops are absolutely creamy and delicious! I can only make them when I have a full house or I'll end up eating them all. My girls especially love this recipe, and they request it on an almost weekly basis.

**YIELD: 6 SERVINGS**

1 tbsp (15 ml) extra-virgin olive oil

1 large sweet onion, sliced

1 clove garlic, minced

2 cups (472 ml) low-sodium chicken broth

3 lb (1.4 kg) frozen bone-in pork chops

2 tbsp (16 g) cornstarch

2 tbsp (30 ml) cold water

8 oz (230 g) sour cream

¼ cup (25 g) grated Parmesan cheese

2 tsp (10 ml) Dijon mustard

½ tsp coarse salt

Freshly ground black pepper

Cooked rice or mashed potatoes, for serving

Press "Saute" to preheat your Instant Pot. When the word "Hot" appears on the display, add the olive oil. When the oil is shimmering, add the onion. Cook until the onion is soft, for about 5 minutes, stirring frequently. Add the garlic and cook for 1 minute.

Add the chicken broth, stirring well to scrape up any browned bits from the bottom. Turn off the Instant Pot.

Add the pork chops to the pot. Close and lock the lid of the Instant Pot. Press "Manual" and immediately adjust the timer to 10 minutes. Check that the cooking pressure is on "High" and that the release valve is set to "Sealing."

When the time is up, open the Instant Pot using "Quick Pressure Release." Remove the pork chops from the pot and set them aside. Press "Cancel," then immediately press "Saute."

Mix together the cornstarch and water. When the liquid is boiling, add the cornstarch "slurry" and stir constantly for at least 1 minute until it's thickened. Stir in the sour cream, Parmesan and Dijon, stirring until smooth. Season with salt and pepper.

Serve the pork chops with the sauce over rice or mashed potatoes.

# BRANDY AU POIVRE RIB-EYE STEAKS

The delicious sauce in this recipe is so good you'll want to drink it. Luckily, it's rich and you don't need a lot to fully enjoy the flavor. This is a great choice to serve for company or a romantic dinner.

**YIELD: 2 TO 3 SERVINGS**

1 tbsp (15 ml) extra-virgin olive oil

2 lb (900 g) frozen rib-eye steaks

½ cup (118 ml) beef broth

1 tbsp (10 g) whole peppercorns, crushed into fine pieces

¼ cup (59 ml) brandy or cognac

¾ cup (177 ml) heavy cream

2 tbsp (28 g) unsalted butter, cut into two pieces

½ tsp coarse salt (or to taste)

Mashed potatoes, for serving

Press "Saute" to preheat your Instant Pot. When the word "Hot" appears on the display, add the olive oil. When the oil is shimmering, add the steaks and cook until they're browned, for about 3 to 4 minutes per side. Turn off the Instant Pot.

Remove the steaks and add the beef broth, scraping up any browned bits from the bottom of the pot. Return the steaks to the pot.

Close and lock the lid of the Instant Pot. Press "Manual" and immediately adjust the timer to 3 minutes. Check that the cooking pressure is on "High" and that the release valve is set to "Sealing."

When the time is up, open the Instant Pot using "Quick Pressure Release." Press "Cancel," then "Saute." Remove the steaks and set them aside. Add the peppercorns and brandy. Boil the liquid until it's reduced by two-thirds, 5 to 7 minutes. Stir in the cream and butter, one piece at a time. Season with salt. Serve the steaks with the sauce and mashed potatoes.

# PORK TENDERLOIN IN GARLIC SAUCE

The fresh herbs in this recipe really infuse the meat as it cooks, turning out a flavorful, tender main dish with very little effort. Feel free to swap in bone-in pork chops for the pork loin if you prefer.

**YIELD: 4 SERVINGS**

2 lb (900 g) frozen pork loin

½ cup (118 ml) low-sodium chicken broth

½ cup (118 ml) dry white wine

1 tbsp (2.5 g) chopped fresh sage

2 tsp (2 g) chopped fresh rosemary

2 sprigs fresh thyme

⅔ cup (150 g) cold unsalted butter, cut into 6 pieces

Salt and pepper, to taste

Place the pork loin, broth, wine, sage, rosemary and thyme in the pot. Close and lock the lid of the Instant Pot. Press "Manual" and immediately adjust the timer to 40 minutes. Check that the cooking pressure is on "High" and that the release valve is set to "Sealing."

When the time is up, allow the pressure to release naturally for 10 minutes, then open the Instant Pot using "Quick Pressure Release." Remove the pork from the pot and set it aside. Skim off the fat from the liquid in the pot and discard. Press "Cancel," then immediately press "Saute." Boil until the liquid in the pot is reduced by one-third, about 5 minutes. Remove the thyme sprigs and discard.

Add the butter, one piece at a time, and stir until each is melted and incorporated into the sauce. Season well with salt and pepper. Slice the pork and serve it with the sauce.

# PINEAPPLE CHIPOTLE RIBS

Before the Instant Pot, the only way I truly enjoyed ribs was either at my favorite barbecue joint or if I cooked them low and slow on my own grill. But the Instant Pot turns out tender, succulent ribs with so little effort that I've taken to making these sweet-spicy ribs even on busy weeknights! Be sure to cut your meat before freezing it (see the tips section on page 7).

**YIELD: 4 TO 6 SERVINGS**

¼ cup (59 ml) apple juice

1 (20-ounce [567-g]) can crushed pineapple, undrained

1 cup (236 ml) prepared barbecue sauce

1–2 chipotle peppers, chopped (from a can of chipotles in adobo sauce)

3 lb (1.4 kg) frozen St. Louis–style pork ribs, cut into 2–3 rib sections

Place the apple juice, pineapple, barbecue sauce and chopped chipotle peppers into the pot (in that order and do not stir). Place the trivet into the pot and carefully place the ribs on top. Close and lock the lid of the Instant Pot. Press "Manual" and immediately adjust the timer to 40 minutes. Check that the cooking pressure is on "High" and that the release valve is set to "Sealing."

When the time is up, allow the pressure to release naturally for 10 minutes, then open the Instant Pot using "Quick Pressure Release." Remove the ribs from the pot and set them aside, then remove the trivet. Return the ribs to the pot and toss them with the sauce.

# MAPLE-MUSTARD PORK RIBS

Whenever the weather gets cooler, I start to crave these ribs. Of course, they're good any time of the year, but the maple flavor goes really well with a side of roasted butternut squash. The Instant Pot turns ribs from frozen to fall-off-the-bone tender while the broiler gives them a nice crispy exterior.

## YIELD: 6 SERVINGS

1 tbsp (15 ml) extra-virgin olive oil

1 large sweet onion, sliced

1 clove garlic, minced

1 cup (236 ml) low-sodium chicken broth

3 lb (1.4 kg) frozen, boneless country-style pork ribs

¼ cup (60 ml) Dijon mustard

¼ cup (60 ml) maple syrup

1 tbsp (9 g) light brown sugar

1 tsp apple cider vinegar

1 tsp Worcestershire sauce

Press "Saute" to preheat your Instant Pot. When the word "Hot" appears on the display, add the olive oil. When the oil is shimmering, add the onion. Cook until the onion is soft, about 5 minutes, stirring frequently. Add the garlic and cook for 1 minute.

Add the chicken broth, stirring well to scrape up any browned bits from the bottom. Turn off the Instant Pot.

Add the pork ribs to the pot. Close and lock the lid of the Instant Pot. Press "Manual" and immediately adjust the timer to 50 minutes. Check that the cooking pressure is on "High" and that the release valve is set to "Sealing."

Meanwhile, mix together the Dijon, maple syrup, brown sugar, apple cider vinegar and Worcestershire sauce and set it aside.

When the time is up, allow the pressure to release naturally. Remove the pork ribs from the pot and place them on a broiler pan. Brush the ribs generously with the sauce. Broil for 4 to 5 minutes or until the sauce is bubbling and the ribs are just starting to brown.

# EFFORTLESS SEAFOOD FEASTS

I used to do a lot of work with the Alaska Seafood Marketing Institute, where I learned that cooking fish straight from frozen is simple to do. Back then, the Instant Pot wasn't around, and I never could have imagined that my straight-from-the-freezer salmon was about to be even easier! I especially love using my Instant Pot for "poaching" frozen salmon because the flavors infuse really nicely.

**MY THREE FAVORITES**
Poached Salmon in Garlic and Wine (page 90)
Easy Shrimp and Sausage Boil (page 92)
Spicy Shrimp Soup (page 98)

# PESTO SALMON

Although this recipe has few ingredients, don't let that fool you. It's packed with flavor! The texture of the breadcrumbs pairs perfectly with the tender, flaky salmon. Using jarred pesto makes it that much simpler and perfect for an easy, delicious weeknight meal.

## YIELD: 4 SERVINGS

½ cup (118 ml) water

4 frozen salmon filets

½ cup (113 g) prepared pesto, at room temperature

2 tbsp (28 ml) melted butter

½ cup (54 g) panko breadcrumbs

Coarse salt and freshly ground black pepper

Add the water to the Instant Pot. Place the trivet in the pot and the salmon on top of the trivet.

Close and lock the lid of the Instant Pot. Press "Manual" and immediately adjust the timer to 5 minutes. Check that the cooking pressure is on "High" and that the release valve is set to "Sealing."

When the time is up, open the Instant Pot using "Quick Pressure Release." Remove the salmon from the pot and set it aside. Place the salmon on a sheet pan, then top with the pesto. Mix together the melted butter and breadcrumbs, then spread that over the top of the pesto.

Broil the salmon until the breadcrumbs are golden brown, for about 2 minutes. Season to taste with salt and pepper.

# SHRIMP SCAMPI

It's never been so simple to make shrimp scampi! Be sure you use the largest shrimp you can find as they can overcook easily. I like to serve this buttery, garlicky shrimp with a side of angel hair pasta and a crusty bread to soak up the flavorful sauce.

## YIELD: 4 SERVINGS

2 tsp (10 ml) extra-virgin olive oil

1 medium shallot, minced

6 cloves garlic, minced

⅓ cup (80 ml) dry white wine

2 lb (900 g) peeled and deveined frozen jumbo shrimp

½ cup (114 g) unsalted butter, cut into 8 pieces

Juice from ½ lemon

¼ cup (10 g) chopped parsley

Coarse salt and freshly ground black pepper

Press "Saute" on the Instant Pot. When the word "Hot" appears on the display, add the oil, then the shallot. Sauté until the shallot starts to soften, for about 3 to 4 minutes. Add the garlic and sauté for 1 minute, stirring frequently. Turn off the Instant Pot.

Pour in the wine. Place the frozen shrimp in a steamer basket and place it in the Instant Pot.

Close and lock the lid of the Instant Pot. Press "Manual" and immediately adjust the timer to 1 minute. Check that the cooking pressure is on "High" and that the release valve is set to "Sealing."

When the time is up, open the Instant Pot using "Quick Pressure Release." Remove the shrimp from the pot and set them aside. Press "Cancel," then immediately press "Saute." Boil the liquid in the pot until it reduces by half, for about 3 to 4 minutes. Add the butter one piece at a time and stir continually until melted. Stir in the lemon juice and parsley, then season with salt and pepper. Add the shrimp back to the pot briefly to reheat.

# POACHED SALMON IN GARLIC AND WINE

The Instant Pot is the perfect vessel to poach salmon, and garlic and wine are the perfect ingredients to add flavor. If you're a garlic lover, feel free to increase the amounts by as much as double. This easy dish is wonderful with a side of roasted asparagus and rice.

**YIELD: 4 SERVINGS**

¼ cup (59 ml) chicken broth

¼ cup (59 ml) fresh lemon juice

½ cup (118 ml) dry white wine

1–2 cloves garlic, minced

1 lb (454 g) frozen salmon filets

2 tbsp (28 g) cold unsalted butter, cut into 4 pieces

¼ cup (10 g) chopped fresh tarragon

Coarse salt and freshly ground black pepper

Cooked rice, for serving

Add the chicken broth, lemon juice, wine and garlic to the Instant Pot, then place the salmon directly in the liquid.

Close and lock the lid of the Instant Pot. Press "Manual" and immediately adjust the timer to 5 minutes. Check that the cooking pressure is on "High" and that the release valve is set to "Sealing."

When the time is up, open the Instant Pot using "Quick Pressure Release." Remove the salmon from the pot and set it aside. Press "Cancel," then immediately press "Saute." Boil until the liquid in the pot is reduced and thickened, for about 5 minutes.

Add the butter one piece at a time and stir continuously until melted. Stir in the tarragon.

Return the salmon to the sauce briefly to reheat. Season to taste with salt and pepper. Serve the salmon with the sauce and a side of cooked rice.

# SHRIMP CAULIFLOWER RICE

Cauliflower rice has reached its peak of popularity, and I've officially jumped on board. I like to buy a big bag of frozen cauliflower rice at Costco and use it in any number of recipes. This particular recipe is creamy and indulgent, and you'll never believe you're not eating regular rice! Note: "0 minutes" is not a typo; you're just bringing the pot to pressure.

**YIELD: 4 SERVINGS**

1 tbsp (15 ml) extra-virgin olive oil

¼ medium onion, chopped

3 cloves garlic, minced

¼ cup (59 ml) fresh lemon juice

¼ cup (59 ml) dry white wine

4 cups (720 g) frozen cauliflower rice

1 lb (454 g) frozen large shrimp

½ cup (118 ml) heavy cream

¼ cup (25 g) grated Parmesan cheese

2 tbsp (5 g) chopped parsley

Coarse salt and freshly ground black pepper

Press "Saute" on the Instant Pot. When the word "Hot" appears on the display, add the oil, then the onion. Sauté until the onion starts to soften, for about 5 minutes. Add the garlic and sauté for 1 more minute, stirring frequently. Turn off the Instant Pot.

Pour in the lemon juice and wine. Add the cauliflower rice, then the shrimp. Close and lock the lid of the Instant Pot. Press "Manual" and immediately adjust the timer to 0 minutes. Check that the cooking pressure is on "High" and that the release valve is set to "Sealing."

When the time is up, open the Instant Pot using "Quick Pressure Release." Remove the shrimp from the pot and set them aside. Press "Cancel," then immediately press "Saute." Add the cream and boil the liquid in the pot until it reduces by half, for about 3 to 4 minutes. Add the Parmesan cheese and parsley, then season with salt and pepper. Add the shrimp back to the pot briefly to reheat.

# EASY SHRIMP AND SAUSAGE BOIL

My family and I absolute LOVE this easy recipe! It makes a lot, has tons of flavor and is so fun to eat. I like to put down newspaper when serving since it can get deliciously messy. The first time I made it, our lively table grew quiet as we were too busy enjoying ourselves. Although a side dish isn't needed here, you might want to have crusty bread on hand to soak up some of the delicious sauce.

**YIELD: 4 SERVINGS**

### FOR THE MAIN DISH

4 cups (946 ml) chicken broth

1 lb (454 g) frozen smoked sausage

4 ears corn, cut into 9 pieces total

1 lb (454 g) baby red potatoes, about 1 inch (2.5 cm) (cut in half if large)

1 tbsp (8 g) Old Bay seasoning

1 lb (454 g) large, frozen easy-peel shrimp

### FOR THE SAUCE

½ cup (114 g) butter

4 cloves garlic, minced

1 tsp Old Bay seasoning

¼ cup (59 ml) fresh lemon juice

¼ cup (10 g) chopped parsley

Coarse salt and freshly ground black pepper

Put the broth, sausage, corn, potatoes and Old Bay seasoning into the Instant Pot.

Close and lock the lid of the Instant Pot. Press "Manual" and immediately adjust the timer to 8 minutes. Check that the cooking pressure is on "High" and that the release valve is set to "Sealing."

When the time is up, open the Instant Pot using "Quick Pressure Release." Immediately add the shrimp to the pot, gently stir and replace the cover. Keep covered for about 5 minutes, or until the shrimp are cooked through (the time will depend on the size of your shrimp). Remove the sausage, corn, potatoes and shrimp from the pot and place them in a large serving bowl, discarding the liquid.

To make the sauce, press "Cancel," then "Saute" on the Instant Pot and add the butter. Once melted, add the garlic and cook for 1 to 2 minutes. Add the Old Bay seasoning, lemon juice and parsley. Season with salt and pepper.

Pour the sauce over the shrimp boil in the bowl. Serve immediately.

# SHRIMP WITH GREEN SAUCE

This recipe is one I've been making for years and the Instant Pot has made it even faster and easier. The sauce is simple but to die for! The parsley and garlic add so much flavor, there's no need for butter or cream. This is another dish that works well with some bread to sop up the extra sauce. Note: "0 minutes" is not a typo; you're just bringing the pot to pressure.

**YIELD: 4 SERVINGS**

⅓ cup (78 ml) olive oil

5 cloves garlic, peeled

1 cup (40 g) parsley

2 green onions, chopped

½ cup (118 ml) dry white wine

1 lb (454 g) frozen peeled and deveined large shrimp

Coarse salt and freshly ground black pepper

Put the olive oil in a high-powered blender, followed by the garlic, parsley and green onions. Blend on high speed until smooth. Set it aside.

Pour the wine into the Instant Pot. Place the frozen shrimp in a steamer basket and place it in the Instant Pot.

Close and lock the lid of the Instant Pot. Press "Manual" and immediately adjust the timer to 0 minutes. Check that the cooking pressure is on "High" and that the release valve is set to "Sealing."

When the time is up, open the Instant Pot using "Quick Pressure Release." Remove the shrimp from the pot and set them aside. Press "Cancel," then immediately press "Saute." Boil the liquid in the pot until it reduces by half, for about 3 to 4 minutes. Add the parsley sauce to the pot and stir occasionally until it's very hot. Add the shrimp back to the pot briefly to reheat. Season to taste with salt and pepper.

# SALMON WITH BASIL SAUCE

This basil sauce would also go wonderfully with any whitefish you have on hand. I've also mixed together butter and breadcrumbs and sprinkled it over the top as I do in the Pesto Salmon (page 86) recipe. It's a delicious recipe that's incredibly versatile!

**YIELD: 4 SERVINGS**

2 cloves garlic, minced

½ cup (118 ml) dry white wine

4 frozen salmon filets

2 tbsp (30 ml) Dijon mustard

¼ cup (59 ml) heavy cream

2 tbsp (28 g) butter, cut into 4 pieces

¼ cup (10 g) chopped fresh basil

Coarse salt and freshly ground black pepper

Add the garlic and wine to the Instant Pot. Place the trivet in the pot and the salmon on the trivet.

Close and lock the lid of the Instant Pot. Press "Manual" and immediately adjust the timer to 5 minutes. Check that the cooking pressure is on "High" and that the release valve is set to "Sealing."

When the time is up, open the Instant Pot using "Quick Pressure Release." Remove the salmon and the trivet from the pot and set the salmon aside. Press "Cancel," then immediately press "Saute." Boil the liquid in the pot until it reduces by half, for about 5 minutes. Stir in the Dijon and cream. Add the butter one piece at a time and stir continuously until melted. Stir in the basil, then season with salt and pepper. Pour the sauce over the salmon and serve.

# SPICY SHRIMP SOUP

I'm a lover of all things spicy, and this shrimp soup is easily one of my favorite soup recipes. And who doesn't love being able to toss their shrimp in frozen after saving so much time making the soup itself? In place of the canned corn, you can add some frozen corn to the soup when you add the shrimp, if you have some on hand.

**YIELD: 6 TO 8 SERVINGS**

2 tsp (10 ml) extra-virgin olive oil

½ medium onion, chopped

1 poblano pepper, chopped

1 celery stalk, diced

1 carrot, peeled and diced

4 cloves garlic, minced

½ tsp dried oregano

½ tsp chipotle powder

1 tsp ground coriander

1 tsp ground cumin

2 tbsp (30 ml) adobo sauce (from a can of chipotles in adobo sauce)

4 cups (946 ml) chicken broth

1 (14.5-oz [411-g]) can fire-roasted diced tomatoes, with liquid

1 (15-oz [432-g]) can fire-roasted corn

1 lb (454 g) medium frozen shrimp

¼ cup (10 g) chopped cilantro

Juice of ½ lime

Coarse salt and freshly ground black pepper

Press "Saute" to preheat your Instant Pot. When the word "Hot" appears on the display, add the olive oil. When the oil is shimmering, add the onion, poblano pepper, celery and carrot and cook until the onion is soft, for about 5 minutes, stirring frequently. Add the garlic, oregano, chipotle powder, coriander and cumin and cook for 1 more minute. Turn off the Instant Pot.

Add the adobo sauce and chicken broth, stirring well to scrape up any browned bits from the bottom. Add the tomatoes and corn to the pot. Close and lock the lid of the Instant Pot. Press "Manual" and immediately adjust the timer to 20 minutes. Check that the cooking pressure is on "High" and that the release valve is set to "Sealing."

When the time is up, open the Instant Pot using "Quick Pressure Release." Press "Cancel," then immediately press "Saute." Add the shrimp and simmer until cooked through, for a few minutes. Add the cilantro and lime juice. Taste, then season with salt and pepper.

*See photo on page 84.

# SALMON BURGERS WITH LEMON-MINT YOGURT SAUCE

These simple salmon "burgers" are a wonderfully light meal with bright, fresh flavors. They're a great way to get more fish in your diet without compromising flavor, and the Instant Pot makes it a breeze!

**YIELD: 4 SERVINGS**

## FOR THE SALMON

½ cup (118 ml) low-sodium chicken broth

¼ cup (59 ml) fresh lemon juice

4 frozen salmon filets

## FOR THE SAUCE

¼ cup (59 g) mayonnaise

½ cup (100 g) Greek yogurt

½ cup (66 g) diced cucumber

2 tsp (30 ml) fresh lemon juice

1 tsp lemon zest

1 tbsp (2.5 g) minced fresh mint

½ tsp coarse salt

¼ tsp freshly ground black pepper

## FOR ASSEMBLY

1 French baguette, cut into 4 pieces

1 medium tomato, sliced

½ cup (10 g) arugula

Add the chicken broth and lemon juice to the Instant Pot, then place the salmon directly in the liquid.

Close and lock the lid of the Instant Pot. Press "Manual" and immediately adjust the timer to 5 minutes. Check that the cooking pressure is on "High" and that the release valve is set to "Sealing."

Meanwhile, to make the sauce, mix together the mayonnaise, yogurt, cucumber, lemon juice and zest, mint, salt and pepper and set it aside.

When the time is up, open the Instant Pot using "Quick Pressure Release." Remove the salmon from the pot. Top each baguette with a salmon filet, sauce, tomato and arugula.

# HEARTY SOUPS AND SALADS

This chapter is easily my favorite. I absolutely adore making soups in my Instant Pot! Frozen meats work especially well in soups as the liquid helps it to become especially tender. Try using frozen meats in almost any soup recipe you find for the Instant Pot. You'll be amazed at how fall-apart tender it becomes.

**MY THREE FAVORITES**
Spicy Sausage, Spinach and White Bean Soup (page 102)
Chicken and Wild Rice Soup (page 116)
Lasagna Soup (page 119)

# SPICY SAUSAGE, SPINACH AND WHITE BEAN SOUP

Although this is one of the quickest meals you can make in your Instant Pot, it's also one of the most flavorful. It's incredibly versatile—use kale or swiss chard instead of the spinach, and any type of flavorful sausage works well.

## YIELD: 8 SERVINGS

1 large onion, chopped

6 cloves garlic, minced

1 tsp paprika

1 tsp smoked paprika

½ cup (118 ml) dry white wine

4 cups (950 ml) chicken stock or broth

1 lb (454 g) frozen spicy Italian sausage links

2 (15.5-oz [439-g]) cans white beans, rinsed and drained

2 (14.5-oz [411-g]) cans fire-roasted diced tomatoes, with liquid

6 cups (180 g) baby spinach leaves

1–2 tsp (2.5–5 g) coarse salt, to taste

1 tbsp (15 ml) fresh lemon juice, or to taste (optional)

Press "Saute" to preheat your Instant Pot. When the word "Hot" appears on the display, add the onion. Cook the onion until it's starting to soften, for about 4 to 5 minutes. Add the garlic, paprika and smoked paprika and cook for 1 minute, stirring frequently.

Add the white wine to deglaze the pot, stirring to scrape up any browned bits from the bottom. Cook until the liquid has almost completely evaporated, for about 4 to 5 minutes. Turn off the Instant Pot.

Pour the chicken stock into the Instant Pot and stir well. Add the sausages, then the white beans and tomatoes. Close and lock the lid of the Instant Pot. Press "Manual" and immediately adjust the timer to 20 minutes. Check that the cooking pressure is on "High" and that the release valve is set to "Sealing."

When the time is up, open the Instant Pot using "Quick Pressure Release." Turn off the Instant Pot, then immediately press "Saute." When the soup comes to a strong simmer (this will happen almost immediately), add the spinach leaves and stir until they're wilted. Season generously with coarse salt. Stir in the lemon juice if you'd like, to "brighten" the flavor.

# CHOPPED THAI SALAD WITH MANGO CHICKEN

This is my favorite salad for weekday lunches to keep me going full-speed. Mix the "dry" salad ingredients together and just top it with the mango and dressing when you're ready for a truly delicious, satisfying lunch. The exotic flavors of this salad will make you look forward to your workweek!

**YIELD: 4 SERVINGS**

1 (15-oz [425-g]) can chopped mangoes, drained and juice reserved

2 large frozen boneless, skinless chicken breasts (about 1 lb [450 g] each to total 2 lb [900 g])

1 (13.5-oz [900-g]) can coconut milk

¼ cup (64 g) creamy peanut butter

1 tbsp (6 g) yellow curry powder

1 clove garlic, minced

1 lime, juiced

1–2 tsp (5–10 ml) Sriracha

1 tsp kosher salt and pepper to taste

4 cups (268 g) chopped kale

2 cups (178 g) chopped cabbage

1 red bell pepper, chopped

1 cup (110 g) shredded carrots

½ cup (72 g) chopped peanuts

½ cup (8 g) chopped cilantro

Set the mango aside and add enough water to the reserved mango juice to equal 1 cup (240 ml) of liquid, then add this to your Instant Pot. Place the frozen chicken directly in the liquid.

Close and lock the lid of the Instant Pot. Press "Manual" and immediately adjust the timer to 12 minutes. Check that the cooking pressure is on "High" and that the release valve is set to "Sealing."

When the time is up, open the Instant Pot using "Quick Pressure Release." Turn off the Instant Pot, discard the liquid and place the chicken breasts on a cutting board. Chop the chicken into small pieces then set it aside.

Wipe out the inner pot and press "Saute." Add the coconut milk, peanut butter, curry powder, garlic, lime juice and Sriracha to the pan. Bring the mixture to a boil then simmer until it's reduced and thickened, for about 10 minutes. Set the dressing aside to cool to room temperature.

Place the kale and cabbage into a large salad bowl and toss it gently to combine. Top with the chicken, reserved mango, bell pepper, carrots, peanuts and cilantro. Season to taste with salt and pepper. Serve with the dressing on the side.

# SAUSAGE PEPPER SOUP WITH CAULIFLOWER RICE

This soup is a great example of how versatile cauliflower rice can be. It looks and tastes so similar to "regular" rice that if you don't tell, no one will be able to tell the difference! I love that I can get extra veggies in without any extra effort.

**YIELD: 6 TO 8 SERVINGS**

2 tsp (10 ml) extra-virgin olive oil

2 bell peppers, chopped (any color)

1 medium yellow onion, chopped

3 cloves garlic, minced

1 tsp dried basil

1 tsp dried oregano

1 tbsp (16 g) tomato paste

4 cups (944 ml) chicken broth

1 lb (454 g) frozen Italian chicken sausage links

1 (16-oz [454-g]) can tomato sauce

2 (14.5-oz [411-g]) cans fire-roasted diced tomatoes, with liquid

2 cups (227 g) frozen cauliflower rice

Coarse salt and freshly ground black pepper

Press "Saute" to preheat your Instant Pot. Add the oil. When the oil is shimmering, add the bell peppers and onion and cook until the onion is soft, for about 5 minutes, stirring frequently. Add the garlic, basil and oregano and cook for 1 minute. Add the tomato paste and cook 1 minute more, stirring frequently. Turn off Instant Pot.

Whisk the chicken broth into the pot and stir to scrape up anything sticking to the bottom of the pot. Add the sausage links, tomato sauce, diced tomatoes and cauliflower rice; stir well. Close and lock the lid of the Instant Pot. Press "Manual" and immediately adjust the timer to 15 minutes. Check that the cooking pressure is on "High" and that the release valve is set to "Sealing."

When time is up, open the Instant Pot using "Quick Pressure Release." Season generously with salt and pepper to taste, and serve.

# TOMATO AND TORTELLINI SOUP

Tomato soup is one of my favorite comfort foods, and it's the first recipe I ever learned from my mom. Adding some frozen tortellini makes it an instant meal. Make a simple salad to have on the side, or if you're really hungry, add grilled cheese with good artisan bread for dipping.

**YIELD: 4 TO 6 SERVINGS**

1 tbsp (15 ml) extra-virgin olive oil

1 medium sweet onion, chopped

4 cloves garlic, minced

½ tsp dried oregano

½ tsp dried basil

4 cups (946 ml) low-sodium chicken broth

1 (12-oz [340-g]) frozen package cheese tortellini

1 (8-oz [226-g]) can tomato sauce

1 (28-oz [822-g]) can crushed tomatoes

2 (14.5-oz [411-g]) cans fire-roasted diced tomatoes, with liquid

Coarse salt and freshly ground black pepper

Press "Saute" to preheat your Instant Pot. When the word "Hot" appears on the display, add the olive oil. When the oil is shimmering, add the onion and cook until it's soft, for about 5 minutes, stirring frequently. Add the garlic, oregano and basil and cook for 1 minute. Turn off the Instant Pot.

Add the chicken broth, stirring well to scrape up any browned bits from the bottom. Add the tortellini to the pot, then the tomato sauce and crushed and diced tomatoes; do not stir.

Close and lock the lid of the Instant Pot. Press "Manual" and immediately adjust the timer to 5 minutes. Check that the cooking pressure is on "High" and that the release valve is set to "Sealing."

When the time is up, open the Instant Pot using "Quick Pressure Release." Season well with salt and pepper.

# ITALIAN WEDDING SOUP

We used to visit an Italian restaurant a few times a month, and I always got their Italian Wedding Soup. It's so simple to throw together using my Instant Pot that now I make it at home at least as often. Any size meatballs will work as they hold their shape well in the Instant Pot and only get more tender as they cook.

## YIELD: 6 TO 8 SERVINGS

2 tsp (10 ml) extra-virgin olive oil

½ medium onion, chopped

1 celery stalk, diced

2 carrots, peeled and diced

4 cloves garlic, minced

1 lb (454 g) frozen Italian meatballs

4 cups (946 ml) low-sodium chicken broth

1 cup (113 g) orzo pasta

4 oz (113 g) fresh spinach leaves

Coarse salt and freshly ground black pepper

½ cup (50 g) grated Parmesan cheese

Press "Saute" to preheat your Instant Pot. When the word "Hot" appears on the display, add the olive oil. When the oil is shimmering, add the onion, celery and carrots and cook until the onion is soft, for about 5 minutes, stirring frequently. Add the garlic and cook for 1 minute. Turn off the Instant Pot.

Add the meatballs and broth, stirring well to scrape up any browned bits from the bottom. Close and lock the lid of the Instant Pot. Press "Manual" and immediately adjust the timer to 20 minutes. Check that the cooking pressure is on "High" and that the release valve is set to "Sealing."

When the time is up, open the Instant Pot using "Quick Pressure Release." Press "Cancel," then immediately press "Saute." Add the orzo pasta and simmer for about 8 minutes until al dente. Add the spinach and stir to wilt it. Taste, then season with salt and pepper.

Ladle into bowls and top each with some grated Parmesan cheese.

# BROCCOLI SOUP WITH FETA

Broccoli and feta are two flavors that go so well together. You can reduce the cooking time to 10 to 15 minutes instead of the 20 minutes listed here; I like to cook it longer to allow the flavors to really develop, but it will be delicious either way. Instead of stirring the feta into the soup, you can put it in individual bowls if you prefer.

## YIELD: 8 TO 10 SERVINGS

2 tsp (10 ml) extra-virgin olive oil

1 large onion, chopped

2 cloves garlic, minced

4 cups (946 ml) low-sodium chicken broth

2 lb (900 g) frozen broccoli

2 cups (472 ml) whole milk

4 oz (113 g) crumbled feta cheese

1 tbsp (8 g) cornstarch (optional)

1 tbsp (15 ml) cold water (optional)

Coarse salt and freshly ground black pepper

Press "Saute" to preheat your Instant Pot. When the word "Hot" appears on the display, add the olive oil. When the oil is shimmering, add the onion and cook until it's soft, for about 5 minutes. Add the garlic and cook for 1 minute. Turn off the Instant Pot.

Add the chicken broth and broccoli to the pot. Close and lock the lid of the Instant Pot. Press "Manual" and immediately adjust the timer to 20 minutes. Check that the cooking pressure is on "High" and that the release valve is set to "Sealing."

When the time is up, open the Instant Pot using "Quick Pressure Release." Using an immersion blender, blend the soup until smooth or to your desired consistency. Add the milk and feta cheese, stirring until the feta melts into the soup.

If it's not thick enough, mix together the cornstarch and cold water, bring the soup to a boil, then stir in the "slurry". Taste, then season with salt and pepper.

# STEAK SALAD WITH ROASTED JALAPEÑOS AND CREAMY POBLANO DRESSING

I've never found salad dressings at the store that I really like, so I make my own, which is just fine by me! The buttermilk in this Creamy Poblano Dressing turns it into something really special and is a perfect balance to the spicy jalapeños in this salad.

**YIELD: 4 SERVINGS**

### FOR THE STEAK

2 tsp (10 ml) extra-virgin olive oil

1 lb (454 g) frozen sirloin

½ cup (118 ml) beef broth or water

### FOR THE DRESSING

1 poblano pepper, roasted, peeled and seeded

1 clove garlic

2 tbsp (30 ml) fresh lime juice

¼ cup (10 g) chives

½ cup (20 g) cilantro

½ cup (118 ml) buttermilk

¾ cup (172 g) mayonnaise

Coarse salt and freshly ground black pepper

### FOR THE SALAD

4 jalapeño peppers, roasted until lightly charred, then chopped

Corn

Tomatoes

Red onion

Cilantro

Red bell pepper

Avocado

Romaine lettuce

Press "Saute" to preheat your Instant Pot. When the word "Hot" appears on the display, add the olive oil. When the oil is shimmering, add the sirloin. Brown it well on both sides, 3 to 4 minutes per side, then set it aside.

Turn off the Instant Pot. Add the beef broth to the pot, stirring well to scrape up any browned bits from the bottom. Add the reserved sirloin directly to the liquid in the pot. Close and lock the lid of the Instant Pot. Press "Manual" and immediately adjust the timer to 20 minutes. Check that the cooking pressure is on "High" and that the release valve is set to "Sealing."

Meanwhile, to make the dressing, place the poblano pepper, garlic, lime juice, chives and cilantro into a high-powered blender. Blend until very smooth. Add the buttermilk and mayo, then pulse the mixture just until it's smooth. Season well with salt and pepper.

When the time is up, allow the pressure to release naturally for 10 minutes, then open the Instant Pot using "Quick Pressure Release." Remove the sirloin and shred it with two forks or slice it. Assemble the salad and top with the dressing. Serve immediately.

# BEEF VEGETABLE SOUP WITH BASIL PESTO

This might be a simple vegetable soup, but you can make it so easily using an Instant Pot, not to mention the beef gets amazingly tender in such a short time. I stir in some basil pesto to really give it a flavor kick!

## YIELD: 4 SERVINGS

2 tsp (10 ml) extra-virgin olive oil

1 lb (454 g) frozen sirloin

1 medium onion, chopped

2 celery stalks, chopped

3 large carrots, chopped

2 cloves garlic, minced

½ tsp dried thyme

6 cups (1.4 L) low-sodium beef broth

1 (14.5-oz [411-g]) can fire-roasted diced tomatoes, with liquid

24 oz (681 g) frozen mixed vegetables

½ cup (113 g) prepared basil pesto

Coarse salt and freshly ground black pepper

Press "Saute" to preheat your Instant Pot. When the word "Hot" appears on the display, add the olive oil. When the oil is shimmering, add the sirloin. Brown it well on both sides, 3 to 4 minutes per side, then set it aside.

Add the onion, celery and carrots and cook until the onion is soft, for about 5 minutes, stirring frequently. Add the garlic and thyme and cook for 1 minute. Turn off the Instant Pot.

Add the beef broth, tomatoes and frozen vegetables, stirring well to scrape up any browned bits from the bottom. Close and lock the lid of the Instant Pot. Press "Manual" and immediately adjust the timer to 20 minutes. Check that the cooking pressure is on "High" and that the release valve is set to "Sealing."

When the time is up, allow the pressure to release naturally for 10 minutes, then open the Instant Pot using "Quick Pressure Release." Remove the sirloin and shred it with two forks, then return it to the pot. Stir in the pesto. Taste, then season with salt and pepper.

# CHICKEN AND WILD RICE SOUP

If you like wild rice, you will love this soup! It was originally my mom's recipe but I made some tweaks for personal preference and to make it more Instant Pot–friendly. This soup is so creamy and has wonderful flavor from the wild rice. Starting with frozen chicken breasts means it's simple to make anytime!

**YIELD: 4 SERVINGS**

1 tbsp (15 ml) extra-virgin olive oil

1 lb (454 g) sliced mushrooms

1 medium onion, chopped

2 celery stalks, chopped

2 carrots, chopped

1 clove garlic, minced

½ tsp dried thyme

½ cup (118 ml) dry white wine

3 tbsp (43 g) unsalted butter

3 tbsp (22 g) flour

6 cups (1.4 L) chicken broth

1 cup (140 g) wild rice

2 lb (900 g) frozen boneless, skinless chicken breasts

1 cup (236 ml) heavy cream

Coarse salt and freshly ground black pepper

Press "Saute" to preheat your Instant Pot. When the word "Hot" appears on the display, add the olive oil. When the oil is shimmering, add the mushrooms. Cook until their liquid has been released and almost fully evaporated and the mushrooms are beginning to brown, about 7 to 8 minutes. Add the onion, celery and carrots and cook until the onion is soft, for about 5 minutes, stirring frequently. Add the garlic and thyme and cook for 1 minute. Add the wine and reduce it to about 1 tablespoon (15 ml), about 5 minutes, stirring frequently.

Add the butter and stir until it's melted. Sprinkle the flour into the pot and stir for 1 minute so the flour loses its raw taste. Slowly whisk in the broth, taking care to scrape any brown bits from the bottom of the pot. Turn off the Instant Pot.

Add the rice and chicken. Close and lock the lid of the Instant Pot. Press "Manual" and immediately adjust the timer to 45 minutes. Check that the cooking pressure is on "High" and that the release valve is set to "Sealing."

When the time is up, open the Instant Pot using "Quick Pressure Release." Remove the chicken to a cutting board and cut it into bite-size pieces, then return it to the pot. Stir in the heavy cream. Taste, then season with salt and pepper.

# LASAGNA SOUP

Oh, this soup is so perfect! I love lasagna but rarely want to take the time to make an entire pan. This soup has all the flavors in a fraction of the time! I prefer ricotta cheese but you could top your soup with a little sour cream too.

**YIELD: 4 SERVINGS**

1 tbsp (15 ml) extra-virgin olive oil

1 lb (454 g) sliced mushrooms

1 medium sweet onion, chopped

4 cloves garlic, minced

1 tsp dried oregano

1 tsp dried basil

1 tbsp (16 g) tomato paste

½ cup (118 ml) pinot noir wine

4 cups (946 ml) low-sodium chicken broth

1 (14.5-oz [411-g]) can crushed tomatoes

1 (14.5-oz [411-g]) can fire-roasted diced tomatoes, with liquid

1 lb (454 g) frozen Italian sausage links

2 cups (210 g) rotini pasta

¼ cup (56 g) cream cheese, softened and cut into 8 small pieces

¼ cup (59 ml) heavy cream

¼ cup (10 g) chopped fresh basil

Coarse salt and freshly ground black pepper

1 cup (246 g) whole-milk ricotta cheese

Press "Saute" to preheat your Instant Pot. When the word "Hot" appears on the display, add the olive oil. When the oil is shimmering, add the mushrooms. Cook until their liquid has been released and almost fully evaporated and the mushrooms are beginning to brown, 7 to 8 minutes. Add the onion and cook until it's soft, for about 5 minutes, stirring frequently. Add the garlic, oregano and basil and cook for 1 minute. Add the tomato paste and cook for 1 minute, stirring frequently. Add the wine and reduce it to about 1 tablespoon (15 ml), about 5 minutes, stirring frequently. Turn off the Instant Pot.

Add the chicken broth, stirring well to scrape up any browned bits from the bottom. Add both cans of tomatoes; do not stir. Set the Italian sausage links gently into the liquid.

Close and lock the lid of the Instant Pot. Press "Manual" and immediately adjust the timer to 15 minutes. Check that the cooking pressure is on "High" and that the release valve is set to "Sealing."

When the time is up, open the Instant Pot using "Quick Pressure Release." Remove the sausage links and set them aside to cool slightly. Turn off the Instant Pot, press "Cancel" and then "Saute." Add the noodles, cream cheese and heavy cream and simmer until the pasta is cooked to al dente (time it according to the package directions). Top with the basil. Taste, then season with salt and pepper.

Ladle the soup into bowls and serve with a dollop of ricotta cheese.

# CHEESE AND SPINACH RAVIOLI SOUP

Everyone has a bag of frozen ravioli in their freezer (or is that just me?). I'll use it in any number of recipes or serve it for my girls as-is, but this easy recipe is definitely one of my go-to's. If you don't have spinach ravioli, feel free to use whatever flavor you have on hand.

## YIELD: 4 SERVINGS

2 tsp (10 ml) extra-virgin olive oil

1 medium onion, chopped

2 carrots, diced

1 celery stalk, diced

2 cloves garlic, minced

6 cups (1.4 L) chicken broth

1 (14.5-oz [411-g]) can fire-roasted diced tomatoes

1 (16-oz [900-g]) package frozen cheese and spinach ravioli

4 oz (113 g) spinach leaves

¼ cup (25 g) grated Parmesan cheese

Coarse salt and freshly ground black pepper

Press "Saute" to preheat your Instant Pot. When the word "Hot" appears on the display, add the olive oil. When the oil is shimmering, add the onion, carrots and celery. Cook until the onion is soft, for about 5 minutes, stirring frequently. Add the garlic and cook for 1 minute. Turn off the Instant Pot.

Add the chicken broth, stirring well to scrape up any browned bits from the bottom. Add the tomatoes and ravioli, then stir gently.

Close and lock the lid of the Instant Pot. Press "Manual" and immediately adjust the timer to 3 minutes (or half the time on the package, if that's different). Check that the cooking pressure is on "High" and that the release valve is set to "Sealing."

When the time is up, open the Instant Pot using "Quick Pressure Release." Add the spinach and Parmesan cheese, stirring gently to wilt the spinach. Taste, then season with salt and pepper.

# CHICKEN AND ROASTED RED PEPPER SOUP

I love roasted red pepper soup, but it's never quite enough to fill me up. For this recipe, I've added chicken to make it a bit heartier. A simple salad and crusty bread on the side makes this a wonderful weeknight meal.

## YIELD: 4 TO 6 SERVINGS

2 tbsp (28 g) unsalted butter

1 large onion, chopped

1 celery stalk, chopped

1 large carrot, chopped

3 cloves garlic, minced

2 cups (472 ml) low-sodium chicken broth

1 (24-oz [680-g]) jar fire-roasted red peppers, with liquid

1 (14.5-oz [411-g]) fire-roasted diced tomatoes, with liquid

1 lb (454 g) frozen chicken tenders

1 cup (236 ml) heavy cream

1 tsp coarse salt

½ tsp freshly ground black pepper

¼ cup (10 g) chopped fresh basil

Press "Saute" to preheat your Instant Pot. When the word "Hot" appears on the display, add the butter. When the butter is almost melted, add the onion, celery and carrot and cook until the onion is soft, for about 5 minutes, stirring frequently. Add the garlic and cook for 1 minute. Add the chicken broth, taking care to scrape any brown bits from the bottom of the pot. Turn off the Instant Pot.

Add the peppers, tomatoes and chicken to the pot. Close and lock the lid of the Instant Pot. Press "Manual" and immediately adjust the timer to 20 minutes. Check that the cooking pressure is on "High" and that the release valve is set to "Sealing."

When the time is up, open the Instant Pot using "Quick Pressure Release." Stir in the heavy cream. Taste, then season with salt and pepper. Top with the fresh basil.

# BEEFY FRENCH ONION SOUP

Onion soup is a perfect go-to since onions are economical and last a long time in the pantry. I like to add beef to mine for an even heartier meal. And since you can add the sirloin to the pot frozen, it's even easier!

## YIELD: 6 TO 8 SERVINGS

2 tsp (10 ml) extra-virgin olive oil

1 lb (450 g) frozen sirloin

¼ cup (57 g) unsalted butter

4 large sweet onions, thickly sliced

3 cloves garlic, minced

½ tsp dried thyme

½ cup (120 ml) dry red wine

8 cups (1.9 L) low-sodium beef broth

1 bay leaf

1 tsp coarse salt

½ tsp freshly ground black pepper

1 small baguette, sliced

2 cups (224 g) shredded Swiss or Gruyère cheese

Press "Saute" to preheat your Instant Pot. When the word "Hot" appears on the display, add the olive oil. When the oil is shimmering, add the frozen sirloin and cook on both sides until browned, 3 to 4 minutes per side. Remove the sirloin and set it aside.

Add the butter and onions to the pot, stirring well to scrape up any browned bits from the bottom. Cook until the onions are lightly golden and caramelized, for about 20 minutes (turn the heat to low if they start to brown too quickly). Add the garlic and thyme to the onions and cook for 1 more minute.

Add the wine to the pot and cook, stirring frequently, until it's almost completely evaporated, about 5 minutes. Add the beef broth to the pot, stirring to scrape up any browned bits from the bottom. Return the reserved sirloin to the pot and add the bay leaf.

Close and lock the lid of the Instant Pot. Press "Manual" and immediately adjust the timer to 20 minutes. Check that the cooking pressure is on "High" and that the release valve is set to "Sealing."

When the time is up, open the Instant Pot using "Quick Pressure Release." Remove the sirloin from the pot and chop it, then return it to the soup. Remove and discard the bay leaf, then season the soup to taste with salt and pepper.

When you're ready to serve the soup, place the baguette slices on a sheet pan and sprinkle evenly with the shredded cheese. Broil until the cheese is melted and the bread is starting to brown. Ladle the soup into bowls and top with a cheesy baguette slice.

# LEMON CHICKEN SOUP WITH CAULIFLOWER RICE

*Avgolemono* is a Greek lemon chicken soup that I absolutely adore. This soup is very similar but I use cauliflower rice in place of regular rice or orzo pasta. You won't be able to tell the difference and you'll get extra veggies too.

## YIELD: 4 SERVINGS

¼ cup (57 g) unsalted butter

½ medium sweet onion, chopped

½ tsp dried oregano

1 carrot, diced

1 celery stalk, diced

3 tbsp (22 g) flour

6 cups (1.4 L) chicken broth

1 lb (454 g) frozen chicken breasts

6 large egg yolks

½ cup (118 ml) fresh lemon juice

2 cups (227 g) frozen cauliflower rice

Coarse salt and freshly ground black pepper

Press "Saute" to preheat your Instant Pot. When the word "Hot" appears on the display, add the butter. When the butter is melted, add the onion, oregano, carrot and celery and cook until the onion is soft, for about 5 minutes, stirring frequently. Add the flour and cook for 1 minute. Turn off the Instant Pot.

Add the chicken broth, stirring well to scrape up any browned bits from the bottom. Add the chicken breasts.

Close and lock the lid of the Instant Pot. Press "Manual" and immediately adjust the timer to 15 minutes. Check that the cooking pressure is on "High" and that the release valve is set to "Sealing."

When the time is up, open the Instant Pot using "Quick Pressure Release." Remove the chicken and set it aside to cool slightly, then chop or shred it. Place the egg yolks in a small bowl and add a few tablespoons of the hot liquid at a time, stirring constantly, until you've added about ½ cup (118 ml) or so. Add the chicken and the egg yolk mixture back into the liquid in the pot. Add the lemon juice and cauliflower rice. Close the lid of the Instant Pot and allow the mixture to sit for 5 minutes. Taste and season with salt and pepper.

# CHICKEN MINESTRONE

The Instant Pot turns what used to take me hours to simmer into something I can make in no time flat. I use jarred marinara and pesto in this minestrone recipe to really speed things up, and starting with frozen chicken makes it a hearty meal that can be made with almost zero prep!

**YIELD: 4 TO 6 SERVINGS**

1 tbsp (15 ml) extra-virgin olive oil

1 large onion, chopped

2 carrots, chopped

2 celery stalks, chopped

3 cloves garlic, minced

4 cups (946 ml) low-sodium chicken broth

1 (15.5-oz [439-g]) can kidney beans, drained

1 lb (454 g) frozen chicken tenders

1 (16-oz [454-g]) package frozen green beans

1 (24-oz [680-g]) jar marinara sauce

1 cup (105 g) dried ditalini pasta

½ tsp crushed red pepper flakes

¼ cup (56 g) prepared pesto

¼ cup (45 g) grated Parmesan cheese

1 tsp coarse salt and freshly ground black pepper (or to taste)

Press "Saute" to preheat your Instant Pot. When the word "Hot" appears on the display, add the olive oil. When the oil is shimmering, add the onion, carrots and celery and cook until the onion is soft, for about 5 minutes, stirring frequently. Add the garlic and cook for 1 minute. Turn off the Instant Pot.

Add the chicken broth, stirring well to scrape up any browned bits from the bottom. Add the kidney beans, chicken, green beans and marinara to the pot.

Close and lock the lid of the Instant Pot. Press "Manual" and immediately adjust the timer to 20 minutes. Check that the cooking pressure is on "High" and that the release valve is set to "Sealing."

When the time is up, open the Instant Pot using "Quick Pressure Release." Remove the chicken tenders and chop or shred them, then return them to the pot. Press "Cancel" and then "Saute." Add the pasta, red pepper flakes and pesto and simmer until the pasta is cooked to al dente (timed according to package directions). Stir in the Parmesan cheese. Taste, then season with salt and pepper.

# BALSAMIC AND DIJON POTATO SALAD WITH SAUSAGE

I absolutely love the flavor combination of balsamic and Dijon, and it's a perfect blend for an upscale potato salad! Italian sausage and balsamic also go wonderfully together, and its addition here elevates the humble potato salad from side to main dish. You can serve this potato salad as soon as it's ready or chill it to take to a potluck to impress your friends.

**YIELD: 4 TO 6 SERVINGS**

1½ cups (354 ml) low-sodium chicken broth

½ lb (227 g) frozen Italian sausage links

1½ lb (680 g) red potatoes, halved (or quartered if large)

¼ cup (60 ml) bottled balsamic glaze

¼ cup (60 ml) extra-virgin olive oil

2 tbsp (30 ml) Dijon mustard

2 celery stalks, diced

2 cloves garlic, minced

½ tsp coarse salt

Freshly ground black pepper

Pour the chicken broth into the bottom of the pot. Add the sausage and potatoes. Close and lock the lid of the Instant Pot. Press "Manual" and immediately adjust the timer to 15 minutes. Check that the cooking pressure is on "High" and that the release valve is set to "Sealing."

Meanwhile, mix together the balsamic glaze, olive oil, Dijon, celery, garlic, salt and pepper for the dressing; set it aside.

When the time is up, open the Instant Pot using "Quick Pressure Release." Carefully remove the potatoes and sausage (be careful; there will be a lot of steam and it will be HOT), and set them aside to cool slightly.

When cool enough to handle, cut the sausage into small bite-sized pieces. Toss the potatoes and sausage with the dressing in a serving bowl. Serve warm or at room temperature.

# BBQ CHICKEN SALAD

I love throwing together a quick salad for lunch. Owning an Instant Pot means that I can make this shredded chicken at the beginning of the week in no time flat, then use it all week long in salads like this one. The chicken is also great on buns for a quick lunch!

YIELD: 4 TO 6 SERVINGS

½ cup (118 ml) chicken broth or water

1–2 lb (454–900 g) frozen chicken breast

½ tsp coarse salt

8 oz (226 g) chopped romaine lettuce

¼ small red onion, diced

1 (15-oz [425-g]) can black beans, rinsed and drained

1 (15-oz [425-g]) can fire-roasted corn, drained

20 cherry tomatoes, halved

½ cup (32 g) crushed tortilla chips

¼ cup (10 g) chopped fresh cilantro

¼ cup (58 ml) bottled barbecue sauce

½ cup (118 ml) ranch dressing

Pour the chicken broth into the pot and add the chicken and salt. Close and lock the lid of the Instant Pot. Press "Manual" and immediately adjust the timer to 10 minutes. Check that the cooking pressure is on "High" and that the release valve is set to "Sealing."

Meanwhile, combine the lettuce, onion, beans, corn, tomatoes, tortilla chips and cilantro in a large serving bowl. Make the dressing by mixing together the barbecue sauce and ranch dressing.

When time is up, open the Instant Pot using "Quick Pressure Release." Carefully remove the chicken and cut it into bite-sized pieces. Add the chicken to the salad and top with the dressing.

# LOADED POTATO SOUP WITH SAUSAGE

This loaded potato soup is perfect for the Instant Pot because there's no need to drain or cook the potatoes separately. And the sausage adds the perfect amount of spice! You won't believe how much flavor it has even though you use so few ingredients.

## YIELD: 6 TO 8 SERVINGS

1 tbsp (15 ml) extra-virgin olive oil

½ medium onion, chopped

3 tbsp (22 g) all-purpose flour

4 cups (946 ml) low-sodium chicken broth

3 lb (1.4 kg) red potatoes, quartered

1 lb (454 g) frozen andouille sausage links

1½ cups (170 g) shredded cheddar cheese

2 cups (472 ml) whole milk

Coarse salt and freshly ground black pepper

Press "Saute" to preheat your Instant Pot. When the word "Hot" appears on the display, add the oil. When the oil is shimmering, add the onion and cook until it's soft, for about 5 minutes, stirring frequently. Add the flour and cook for 1 minute, stirring constantly. Add the chicken broth, taking care to scrape any brown bits from the bottom of the pot. Turn off the Instant Pot.

Add the potatoes and sausage links to the pot. Close and lock the lid of the Instant Pot. Press "Manual" and immediately adjust the timer to 20 minutes. Check that the cooking pressure is on "High" and that the release valve is set to "Sealing."

When the time is up, open the Instant Pot using "Quick Pressure Release." Remove the sausage, cut it into bite-sized pieces and return it to the pot. Press "Cancel," then press "Saute." Add the cheese and milk, stirring until the cheese is completely melted and incorporated. Season generously with salt and pepper.

# CREOLE SAUSAGE SOUP

If you don't have creole seasoning on hand, you're going to want to pick some up on your next trip to the store. This wonderful soup is simply delightful, and made even better if you serve it over some rice or cheesy grits.

**YIELD: 6 TO 8 SERVINGS**

1 tbsp (15 ml) extra-virgin olive oil

1 medium onion, chopped

1 medium green pepper, chopped

2 celery stalks, chopped

5 cloves garlic, minced

1 tbsp (8 g) creole seasoning

1 tbsp (16 g) tomato paste

2 cups (472 ml) low-sodium chicken broth

1 (14.5-oz [411-g]) can fire-roasted diced tomatoes, with liquid

1 (15-oz [425-g]) can tomato sauce

1 lb (454 g) frozen andouille sausage links

1 bay leaf

2 tsp (10 ml) fresh lemon juice

2 tsp (10 ml) Worcestershire sauce

½ lb (227 g) frozen shrimp, peeled and deveined (optional)

2 tbsp (5 g) chopped fresh parsley

Coarse salt and freshly ground black pepper

Cooked rice or cheesy grits, for serving

Press "Saute" to preheat your Instant Pot. When the word "Hot" appears on the display, add the olive oil. When the oil is shimmering, add the onion, green pepper and celery and cook until the onion is soft, about 5 minutes, stirring frequently. Add the garlic and creole seasoning and cook for 1 minute. Add the tomato paste and cook for 1 minute, stirring constantly. Remove the insert from the Instant Pot to stop the cooking process and press "Cancel" to turn it off.

Add the chicken broth, stirring well to scrape up any browned bits from the bottom. Add the diced tomatoes, tomato sauce, sausage links and bay leaf to the pot. Return the pot to the base.

Close and lock the lid of the Instant Pot. Press "Manual" and immediately adjust the timer to 20 minutes. Check that the cooking pressure is on "High" and that the release valve is set to "Sealing."

When the time is up, open the Instant Pot using "Quick Pressure Release." Remove the sausage and cut it into bite-sized pieces, then return it to the pot. Press "Cancel", and then "Saute." Add the lemon juice, Worcestershire sauce and shrimp (if using). Simmer until the shrimp are cooked through (time depends on the size of your shrimp). Stir in the parsley. Taste, then season with salt and pepper. Remove the bay leaf and serve the soup over cooked rice or cheesy grits.

# CHEESY MEATBALL SOUP

This soup is a nod to my Wisconsin upbringing. I've always loved cheese soup, and here I've added meatballs to really turn it into a one-pot meal. Be sure to have some bread on hand for dipping, and a simple side salad will balance the rich cheese nicely.

**YIELD: 4 TO 6 SERVINGS**

½ cup (114 g) unsalted butter

2 medium onions, chopped

3 tbsp (22 g) all-purpose flour

5 cups (1.1 L) low-sodium chicken broth

1 lb (454 g) frozen spicy meatballs

5 cups (1.1 L) whole milk

2 lb (900 g) shredded sharp cheddar cheese

1 tsp coarse salt

Freshly ground black pepper

Press "Saute" to preheat your Instant Pot. When the word "Hot" appears on the display, add the butter. When the butter is almost melted, add the onions and cook until the onions are soft, for about 5 minutes, stirring frequently. Add the flour and cook for 1 minute. Add the chicken broth, stirring well to scrape up any browned bits from the bottom, then add the meatballs.

Close and lock the lid of the Instant Pot. Press "Manual" and immediately adjust the timer to 20 minutes. Check that the cooking pressure is on "High" and that the release valve is set to "Sealing."

When the time is up, open the Instant Pot using "Quick Pressure Release." Press "Cancel," and then "Saute." Add the milk, then stir in the cheese about a cup (113 g) at a time, making sure it's melted and incorporated before adding more. Season with salt and pepper.

# BRATWURST AND CARAMELIZED ONION SOUP

And here we have another nod to my home state of Wisconsin. Bratwurst with onions is something I've enjoyed more times than I can count, and this soup allows me to enjoy those flavors even in the middle of the coldest winter. Using the Instant Pot means I don't have to break out my grill, plus it's ready in a fraction of the time!

**YIELD: 6 TO 8 SERVINGS**

¼ cup (57 g) unsalted butter

4 large sweet onions, thickly sliced

6 cups (1.4 L) low-sodium beef broth

1 lb (454 g) frozen bratwurst

2 bay leaves

3 sprigs fresh thyme (plus more for garnishing, if desired)

1 tsp coarse salt

Freshly ground black pepper

2 cups (224 g) shredded Swiss cheese

Press "Saute" to preheat your Instant Pot. When the word "Hot" appears on the display, add the butter. When the butter is almost melted, add the onions and cook until the onions are very soft and starting to caramelize, for about 20 minutes, stirring frequently.

Add the beef broth, stirring well to scrape up any browned bits from the bottom. Add the bratwurst, bay leaves and thyme to the pot.

Close and lock the lid of the Instant Pot. Press "Manual" and immediately adjust the timer to 20 minutes. Check that the cooking pressure is on "High" and that the release valve is set to "Sealing."

When the time is up, open the Instant Pot using "Quick Pressure Release." Remove the bay leaves and thyme sprigs and discard them. Remove the bratwurst and cut it into bite-sized pieces, then return it to the pot. Season with salt and pepper. Top each bowl with some shredded Swiss cheese and a thyme sprig, if desired.

# PEA SOUP WITH LEMON AND FETA

This soup is one of my favorites for its simplicity. It's so quick to make yet has so much flavor! I love that I can get the remaining ingredients ready in the time it takes to cook the peas in my Instant Pot.

**YIELD: 4 SERVINGS**

2 cups (472 ml) low-sodium chicken broth

1 (32-oz [908-g]) bag frozen peas

⅓ cup (78 ml) extra-virgin olive oil

2 tsp (10 ml) fresh lemon juice

1 tsp coarse salt and freshly ground black pepper (or to taste)

½ cup (76 g) crumbled feta cheese, for serving

Add the chicken broth and peas to the pot. Close and lock the lid of the Instant Pot. Press "Manual" and immediately adjust the timer to 2 minutes. Check that the cooking pressure is on "High" and that the release valve is set to "Sealing."

When the time is up, open the Instant Pot using "Quick Pressure Release." Using an immersion blender, slowly drizzle in the oil while pureeing the peas until smooth. Add the lemon juice and season with salt and pepper. Top each bowl with some crumbled feta cheese.

# HAM AND SPLIT PEA SOUP

We make ham often , and I always save the ham bone in the freezer. This recipe used to take me several hours, but now it's done in practically no time at all and skips all the stirring!

**YIELD: 6 TO 8 SERVINGS**

2 tsp (10 ml) extra-virgin olive oil

1 large onion, chopped

2 celery stalks, chopped

2 carrots, chopped

1½ tsp (2 g) dried thyme

⅛ tsp dried marjoram

1 lb (454 g) dried split peas

8 cups (1.9 L) water

1 small to medium frozen ham bone

1 large potato, chopped

2 tbsp (30 ml) dry sherry

1 tsp coarse salt

½ tsp freshly ground black pepper

Press "Saute" to preheat your Instant Pot. When the word "Hot" appears on the display, add the olive oil. When the oil is shimmering, add the onion, celery and carrots and cook until the onion is soft, for about 5 minutes, stirring frequently. Add the thyme and marjoram and cook for 1 more minute. Turn off the Instant Pot.

Add the dried split peas and the water, stirring well to scrape up any browned bits from the bottom. Set the ham bone and chopped potato in the water. Close and lock the lid of the Instant Pot. Press "Manual" and immediately adjust the timer to 20 minutes. Check that the cooking pressure is on "High" and that the release valve is set to "Sealing."

When the time is up, allow the Instant Pot to release the pressure naturally, then open the pot. Remove the ham bone and set it aside to cool slightly. Puree the soup with an immersion blender until smooth. Remove all the ham from the bone and return the meat to the pot, discarding the bone. Stir in the sherry, salt and pepper.

# BLACK BEAN AND CORN SOUP

Keep canned beans and frozen corn on hand and you can enjoy this soup anytime! You can use dried beans as well; just increase the cooking time to 50 minutes. This is a wonderfully healthy soup with a nice texture from the corn. Normally, you'd have to simmer black bean soup for an hour or longer on the stovetop to get the flavors right, but the Instant Pot melds the flavors together in a fraction of the time!

**YIELD: 6 TO 8 SERVINGS**

1 tbsp (15 ml) extra-virgin olive oil

¼ medium onion, chopped

2 cloves garlic, minced

1 tbsp (8 g) ground cumin

2 cups (472 ml) low-sodium chicken broth

2 (15-oz [425-g]) cans black beans, undrained

3 cups (408 g) frozen corn

¼ cup (10 g) chopped fresh cilantro

½ tsp coarse salt

Freshly ground black pepper

Press "Saute" to preheat your Instant Pot. When the word "Hot" appears on the display, add the oil. When the oil is shimmering, add the onion and cook until the onion is soft, for about 5 minutes, stirring frequently. Add the garlic and cumin and cook for 1 more minute. Turn off the Instant Pot.

Add the chicken broth, stirring well to scrape up any browned bits from the bottom. Add the beans to the pot.

Close and lock the lid of the Instant Pot. Press "Manual" and immediately adjust the timer to 15 minutes. Check that the cooking pressure is on "High" and that the release valve is set to "Sealing."

When the time is up, open the Instant Pot using "Quick Pressure Release." Add the corn and cilantro, allowing the corn to "cook" in the hot soup for a few minutes. Season with salt and pepper.

# BUTTERNUT SQUASH AND SAUSAGE SOUP

This soup is perfect since you can use frozen butternut squash as well as fresh. Garnish it with fresh sage leaves for an especially pretty bowl of soup.

**YIELD: 4 TO 6 SERVINGS**

1 tbsp (15 ml) extra-virgin olive oil

½ medium onion, chopped

1 carrot, chopped

¼ tsp dried thyme

3 cups (472 ml) low-sodium chicken broth

1 lb (454 g) frozen butternut squash

½ lb (227 g) frozen Italian sausage links

½ cup (118 ml) whole milk

½ tsp coarse salt

Freshly ground black pepper

Press "Saute" to preheat your Instant Pot. When the word "Hot" appears on the display, add the oil. When the oil is shimmering, add the onion and carrot and cook until the onion is soft, about 5 minutes, stirring frequently. Add the thyme and cook for 1 minute. Turn off the Instant Pot.

Add the chicken broth, stirring well to scrape up any browned bits from the bottom. Add the butternut squash and sausage links to the pot.

Close and lock the lid of the Instant Pot. Press "Manual" and immediately adjust the timer to 20 minutes. Check that the cooking pressure is on "High" and that the release valve is set to "Sealing."

When the time is up, open the Instant Pot using "Quick Pressure Release." Remove the sausage and cut it into bite-size pieces. Puree the soup using an immersion blender until smooth.

Stir in the milk and return the sausage to the pot. Season with salt and pepper.

# SMOKY HAM AND BEAN SOUP

If you have a frozen ham hock in your freezer, this is the recipe for you! Start saving them after your Easter ham is gone so you can make this delicious soup at a moment's notice. It's a hearty soup that will really fill you up and warm your insides!

**YIELD: 4 TO 6 SERVINGS**

1 tbsp (15 ml) extra-virgin olive oil

1 medium onion, chopped

3 carrots, chopped

1 celery stalk, chopped

2 cloves garlic, minced

½ tsp dried basil

½ tsp dried oregano

8 cups (1.9 L) water

1 lb (454 g) dried white beans

1 meaty frozen ham hock

2 bay leaves

1 tsp coarse salt

Freshly ground black pepper

Press "Saute" to preheat your Instant Pot. When the word "Hot" appears on the display, add the oil. When the oil is shimmering, add the onion, carrots and celery and cook until the onion is soft, for about 5 minutes, stirring frequently. Add the garlic, basil and oregano and cook for 1 minute. Turn off the Instant Pot.

Add the water, stirring well to scrape up any browned bits from the bottom. Add the beans, ham hock and bay leaves to the pot.

Close and lock the lid of the Instant Pot. Press "Manual" and immediately adjust the timer to 30 minutes. Check that the cooking pressure is on "High" and that the release valve is set to "Sealing."

When the time is up, open the Instant Pot using "Quick Pressure Release." Remove the ham hock and bay leaves (discard the bay leaves). Using a potato masher, mash half of the soup for a creamier texture if you'd like. Remove the meat from the hock and return the meat to the soup. Season with salt and pepper.

# SIMPLE, NO-SWEAT SANDWICHES

I almost always keep some kind of sliced meat in our refrigerator for sandwiches during the week. Whether I'm sending one to school with my girls, making a quick lunch for myself while I'm working or we need a quick and easy dinner on the go, it always helps to have some on hand. It's expensive to buy it at the deli counter, however, so now I buy meats when they're on sale and toss them straight from the freezer into my Instant Pot for sandwiches we can eat all week long.

**MY THREE FAVORITES**
Lemon-Pepper Chicken Salad Sandwiches (page 142)
Chicken Sausage and Sweet Onion Sandwiches (page 148)
Salmon BLTs (page 157)

# LEMON-PEPPER CHICKEN SALAD SANDWICHES

I love the lemon-pepper flavor combination, and it's so perfect for these sandwiches! I like to butter and toast the buns—and add bacon, of course! These sandwiches are great to make ahead of time to take on a picnic or serve on mini-croissants for a shower or tea. Though I usually serve the sandwiches while the chicken salad is warm, it can also be refrigerated and served cold, if preferred.

**YIELD: 4 TO 6 SERVINGS**

½ cup (118 ml) chicken stock

2 lb (900 g) frozen chicken breasts

¼ cup (58 g) plain Greek yogurt

½ cup (115 g) mayonnaise

Zest from 1 lemon

½ tsp freshly ground black pepper

½ tsp lemon-pepper seasoning

1 celery stalk, chopped

2 tbsp (5 g) chopped basil

4 to 6 buns, for serving

**OPTIONAL TOPPINGS**

Lettuce

Sliced tomatoes

Crispy bacon

Pour the chicken stock into the Instant Pot, then set the chicken breasts on top.

Close and lock the lid of the Instant Pot. Press "Manual" and immediately adjust the timer to 10 minutes. Check that the cooking pressure is on "High" and that the release valve is set to "Sealing."

Meanwhile, mix together the yogurt, mayo, lemon zest, pepper, lemon-pepper seasoning, celery and basil. Set it aside.

When the time is up, open the Instant Pot using "Quick Pressure Release." Remove the chicken and cut it into bite-sized pieces. Mix the chicken and dressing together. Pile it onto buns with your desired toppings.

# TURKEY AND BRIE BAGUETTES

This sandwich is similar to one I order at a local coffee shop, made better since I can make mine in my Instant Pot and eat it all week long! It's a perfect picnic sandwich since the cheese is better at room temperature.

**YIELD: 6 SERVINGS**

½ cup (118 ml) water or chicken broth

2 lb (900 g) frozen turkey breast

1 French baguette, sliced lengthwise

8 oz (227 g) brie, sliced

1 large green apple, thinly sliced

1 bunch arugula

¼ cup (62 g) whole-grain mustard

Coarse salt and freshly ground black pepper (optional)

Add the water or chicken broth to the pot, then add the frozen turkey breast.

Close and lock the lid of the Instant Pot. Press "Manual" and immediately adjust the timer to 50 minutes. Check that the cooking pressure is on "High" and that the release valve is set to "Sealing."

When the time is up, allow the pressure to release naturally for 10 minutes, then open the Instant Pot using "Quick Pressure Release." Remove the turkey from the pot and slice thinly.

Place the warm turkey onto the sliced baguette, then top with brie, apple, arugula, mustard and salt and pepper (if using). Slice into 6 pieces for serving.

# EASY PHILLY CHEESESTEAKS

There's a local deli here called Balzano's, and there's been a huge debate around whether they make the best cheesesteaks in our area. I say yes, they do, and I have tried to duplicate it here with a recipe I think is pretty close! I highly suggest adding the mushrooms and jalapeño peppers too.

**YIELD: 4 SERVINGS**

2 lb (900 g) frozen boneless rib-eye steaks

1 tsp coarse salt

½ tsp freshly ground black pepper

2 tsp (10 ml) extra-virgin olive oil

1 medium onion, sliced

1 green pepper, sliced

½ cup (118 ml) beef stock

Fresh rolls

Cheese spread (such as Cheez Whiz) or sliced provolone cheese

Sautéed mushrooms (optional)

Jalapeño peppers (optional)

Remove the steaks from freezer and allow them to thaw for 30 minutes. Slice the steaks against the grain very thinly. (Alternatively, if using fresh steaks, freeze for 30 to 60 minutes, then slice.) Season the steaks with salt and pepper.

Press "Saute" to preheat your Instant Pot. When the word "Hot" appears on the display, add the olive oil. When the oil is shimmering, add the onion and the green pepper. Cook until the onion starts to soften, about 5 minutes. Turn off the Instant Pot.

Add the beef stock, stirring well to scrape up any browned bits from the bottom. Add the steaks to the pot. Close and lock the lid of the Instant Pot. Press "Manual" and immediately adjust the timer to 10 minutes. Check that the cooking pressure is on "High" and that the release valve is set to "Sealing."

When the time is up, open the Instant Pot using "Quick Pressure Release." Remove the steaks, pepper and onion from the pot and place them on a cutting board. Chop them into small pieces.

Pile the steak mixture onto the fresh rolls and add the cheese, mushrooms and jalapeños as desired. Drizzle with a little of the liquid from the pot if you like! If adding cheese, melt it briefly under the broiler.

*See photo on page 140.

# STEAK HOUSE SANDWICHES

We love a good steak sandwich. Tender beef, some buttery, toasted bread and a little crumbled blue cheese is what makes it for me. Add a little mustard and mayo, if you like, and it's perfection! The Instant Pot makes the steak so tender that I'll never use my stove or oven again.

**YIELD: 4 SERVINGS**

2 tsp (10 ml) extra-virgin olive oil

1 large sweet onion, sliced

2 cloves garlic, minced

1 tsp steak seasoning

½ cup (118 ml) balsamic vinegar

2 lb (900 g) frozen sirloin steaks

4 buns, toasted, for serving

Crumbled blue cheese

Arugula, for topping

Coarse salt and freshly ground black pepper

Press "Saute" to preheat your Instant Pot. When the word "Hot" appears on the display, add the olive oil. When the oil is shimmering, add the onion. Cook until it's soft, for about 5 minutes, stirring frequently. Add the garlic and steak seasoning and cook for 1 minute.

Add the balsamic vinegar, stirring well to scrape up any browned bits from the bottom. Turn off the Instant Pot.

Add the steak to the pot. Close and lock the lid of the Instant Pot. Press "Manual" and immediately adjust the timer to 15 minutes. Check that the cooking pressure is on "High" and that the release valve is set to "Sealing."

When the time is up, open the Instant Pot using "Quick Pressure Release." Remove the steaks and slice them against the grain. Assemble the sandwiches on toasted buns with blue cheese, arugula and salt and pepper as desired.

# CHICKEN SAUSAGE AND SWEET ONION SANDWICHES

I like to load these sausage sandwiches with lots of brown mustard and pair them with a side of potato chips. It's a great lunch that we like to enjoy on our deck when the weather is nice, or wrap individually in foil to take on a picnic.

**YIELD: 6 SERVINGS**

2 tsp (10 ml) extra-virgin olive oil

2 large sweet onions, sliced

2 cloves garlic, minced

¼ cup (59 ml) chicken broth

1 lb (454 g) frozen chicken sausage links

6 hoagie rolls, buttered and toasted

6 slices Swiss cheese

Brown mustard, for serving, optional

Press "Saute" to preheat your Instant Pot, then set to "low." When the word "Hot" appears on the display, add the olive oil. When the oil is shimmering, add the onions. Cook until the onions are soft and starting to caramelize, for about 10 minutes, stirring frequently. Add the garlic and cook for 1 minute.

Add the chicken broth, stirring well to scrape up any browned bits from the bottom. Turn off the Instant Pot.

Add the chicken sausage links to the pot. Close and lock the lid of the Instant Pot. Press "Manual" and immediately adjust the timer to 10 minutes. Check that the cooking pressure is on "High" and that the release valve is set to "Sealing."

When the time is up, open the Instant Pot using "Quick Pressure Release." Remove the chicken sausage from the pot and set it aside. Press "Cancel," then immediately press "Saute." Boil until the liquid in the pot is reduced and thickened, for about 5 minutes.

Place a chicken sausage and some of the onion "sauce" on a roll. Top it with Swiss cheese and pop it under the broiler to melt. Serve immediately with a squeeze of brown mustard, if desired.

# SHRIMP ROLLS

If you've ever had a lobster roll, this will be familiar to you. If I could have any sandwich for the rest of my life, these Shrimp Rolls would be a top contender. Don't skip buttering and toasting your rolls, as it really makes all the difference! You can also make the shrimp and dressing ahead of time, then mix them together just before serving. Note: "0 minutes" is not a typo; you're just bringing the pot to pressure.

**YIELD: 4 SERVINGS**

½ cup (115 g) mayonnaise

3 tbsp (45 ml) fresh lemon juice

1 celery stalk, minced

2 tbsp (5 g) chopped parsley

1 tbsp (2.5 g) chopped chives

Coarse salt and freshly ground black pepper

1 cup (236 ml) water or chicken broth

1 lb (454 g) frozen peeled and deveined jumbo shrimp

4 hot dog buns, buttered and toasted

Mix together the mayonnaise, lemon juice, celery, parsley and chives. Taste, then season with salt and pepper. Set it aside.

Pour the water or broth into the Instant Pot. Place the frozen shrimp in a steamer basket and place it in the Instant Pot.

Close and lock the lid of the Instant Pot. Press "Manual" and immediately adjust the timer to 0 minutes. Check that the cooking pressure is on "High" and that the release valve is set to "Sealing."

When the time is up, open the Instant Pot using "Quick Pressure Release." Remove the shrimp from the pot and allow them to cool.

Mix the shrimp with the dressing mixture. Pile it onto buttered hot dog buns.

# BBQ BEEF SANDWICHES WITH CRUNCHY SLAW

The beef in these sandwiches is so tender and a perfect match for the crunchy slaw. What normally would take hours in the oven, takes just 45 minutes under pressure to get the same tender, juicy results!

**YIELD: 6 TO 8 SERVINGS**

2 tsp (10 ml) extra-virgin olive oil

2 lb (900 g) frozen chuck roast, cut into 2 pieces

1 medium onion, quartered

1 cup (236 ml) low-sodium beef broth

4 cups (944 ml) barbecue sauce, divided

⅓ cup (79 g) mayonnaise

1 tbsp (15 ml) white vinegar

1 large pinch of sugar

½ tsp coarse salt

Freshly ground black pepper

3 cups (360 g) packaged slaw mix

Toasted buns

Press "Saute" to preheat your Instant Pot, and set to "low." When the word "Hot" appears on the display, add the olive oil. When the oil is shimmering, brown the beef on all sides, 3 to 4 minutes per side, in batches if necessary; then set the beef aside.

Add the onion and beef broth, stirring well to scrape up any browned bits from the bottom. Turn off the Instant Pot.

Return the beef to the pot, then pour 1 cup (236 ml) of the barbecue sauce over the beef. Close and lock the lid of the Instant Pot. Press "Manual" and immediately adjust the timer to 45 minutes. Check that the cooking pressure is on "High" and that the release valve is set to "Sealing."

Meanwhile, mix together the mayo, vinegar, sugar, salt and pepper. Combine that with the slaw mix and set it aside.

When the time is up, allow the pressure to release naturally for 10 minutes, then open the Instant Pot using "Quick Pressure Release." Remove the beef from the pot and shred it with two forks. Mix the beef with the remaining 3 cups (709 ml) of barbecue sauce.

Top each bun with some BBQ beef and slaw.

# CHIPOTLE TURKEY CLUBS

The smoky flavor of chipotle plays so nicely with turkey, especially when you use your Instant Pot to get it so tender. You'll want to keep this easy-to-make turkey on hand for sandwiches all week long!

## YIELD: 6 TO 8 SERVINGS

### FOR THE SANDWICHES

1 cup (236 ml) chicken broth

4 chipotle chiles, chopped (from a can of chipotles in adobo sauce)

2 lb (900 g) frozen turkey breast, cut into 2 pieces

Toasted rolls

### OPTIONAL TOPPINGS

Mayonnaise

Lettuce

Tomato

Swiss cheese

Crispy bacon

Add the chicken broth and chipotle chiles to the pot, then add the frozen turkey breast.

Close and lock the lid of the Instant Pot. Press "Manual" and immediately adjust the timer to 50 minutes. Check that the cooking pressure is on "High" and that the release valve is set to "Sealing."

When the time is up, allow the pressure to release naturally for 10 minutes, then open the Instant Pot using "Quick Pressure Release." Remove the turkey from the pot and slice it thinly. Return the turkey to the pot and toss it with the chipotle broth.

Place a few slices of the warm turkey onto the toasted rolls, then top with mayo, lettuce, tomato, cheese and bacon as desired.

# GARLIC PORK LOIN AND PROSCIUTTO SANDWICHES

The prosciutto in this sandwich makes this dish upscale enough that you could proudly serve it anytime. Pack some up to enjoy at the kid's soccer games and everyone will be drooling! They'd never believe it if you told them how quickly your Instant Pot turned frozen meat into something so delectable.

**YIELD: 4 TO 6 SERVINGS**

### FOR THE SANDWICHES

2 tsp (10 ml) extra-virgin olive oil

10 cloves garlic, smashed

1 cup (236 ml) low-sodium chicken broth

1 lb (454 g) frozen pork loin

Toasted buns

### OPTIONAL TOPPINGS

Thinly sliced prosciutto

Lettuce

Tomato

Mustard

Press "Saute" to preheat your Instant Pot. When the word "Hot" appears on the display, add the olive oil. When the oil is shimmering, add the garlic and sauté until it's just starting to brown, about 1 to 2 minutes.

Add the broth, stirring well to scrape up any browned bits from the bottom. Turn off the Instant Pot. Add the pork loin to the pot.

Close and lock the lid of the Instant Pot. Press "Manual" and immediately adjust the timer to 30 minutes. Check that the cooking pressure is on "High" and that the release valve is set to "Sealing."

When the time is up, allow the pressure to release naturally for 10 minutes, then open the Instant Pot using "Quick Pressure Release." Remove the pork from the pot and slice it. Return the pork to the pot and toss it with the garlic broth.

Place a few slices of the warm pork onto the toasted buns, then top with prosciutto, lettuce, tomato and mustard as desired.

# SALMON BLTS

This sandwich is one that I often order at a local oyster house. At least I used to, before I discovered how easy it is to make it myself using frozen salmon and my Instant Pot! Salmon and bacon go surprisingly well together, and the basil aioli brings it all together.

**YIELD: 4 SERVINGS**

### FOR THE BLT

½ cup (118 ml) low-sodium chicken broth

¼ cup (59 ml) lemon juice

4 (6-oz [170-g]) frozen salmon filets

1 French baguette

### FOR THE BASIL AIOLI

½ cup (120 g) mayonnaise

¼ cup (10 g) finely chopped basil

Zest from 1 lemon

### TOPPINGS

Crispy bacon

Lettuce

Tomato

Add the chicken broth and lemon juice to the Instant Pot, then place the salmon directly in the liquid.

Close and lock the lid of the Instant Pot. Press "Manual" and immediately adjust the timer to 5 minutes. Check that the cooking pressure is on "High" and that the release valve is set to "Sealing."

Meanwhile, mix together the mayo, basil and lemon zest for the basil aioli.

When the time is up, open the Instant Pot using "Quick Pressure Release." Remove the salmon from the pot. Top each baguette with a generous smear of the basil aioli, 1 salmon filet, bacon, lettuce and tomato.

# QUICK AND DELECTABLE SIDE DISHES

Who doesn't have at least a few bags of frozen vegetables in their freezer at any given time? The ease of tossing them into your Instant Pot for a quick side dish just can't be beat. Adding a few flavor twists transforms boring side dishes into something just as impressive as your main dish. The Instant Pot works really well with frozen veggies, and you'll love how they retain their texture and flavor!

**MY THREE FAVORITES**
Creamed Corn with Bacon Breadcrumbs (page 160)
Parmesan Corn over Broiled Ricotta (page 163)
Mushy Peas with Fresh Mint (page 167)

# CREAMED CORN WITH BACON BREADCRUMBS

My mom loves this dish so much that she asks me to bring it to every holiday and other type of gathering she hosts! It's creamed corn but with a wonderful flavor and texture from the bacon breadcrumb topping.

**YIELD: 6 TO 8 SERVINGS**

4 strips bacon, sliced crosswise into 1-inch (2.5-cm) pieces

1 medium onion, chopped

¼ cup (59 ml) chicken broth

4 cups (656 g) frozen corn

¼ cup (25 g) grated Parmesan cheese

½ cup (54 g) panko breadcrumbs

¼ cup (57 g) butter, melted

¾ cup (177 ml) heavy cream

¼ cup (58 g) cream cheese, softened

½ tsp coarse salt

Press "Saute" to preheat your Instant Pot. When the word "Hot" appears on the display, add the bacon and cook until the fat has rendered and the bacon is crispy. Remove the bacon with a slotted spoon and set it on paper towels to drain the grease.

Add the onion to the grease in the pot, stirring to scrape up the brown bits from the bottom. Cook the onion for about 4 to 5 minutes or until it's soft. Turn off the Instant Pot.

Add the chicken broth and stir well. Add the corn; do not stir.

Press "Manual" and immediately adjust the timer to 1 minute. Check that the cooking pressure is on "High" and that the release valve is set to "Sealing."

Meanwhile, crumble or finely chop the bacon. Mix the bacon with the Parmesan cheese, panko breadcrumbs and melted butter, then set it aside.

When the time is up, open the Instant Pot using "Quick Pressure Release." Press "Cancel," then immediately press "Saute." Add the heavy cream, cream cheese and salt. Gently boil the mixture until it's thickened and the cream cheese is completely incorporated, for about 5 minutes.

Pour the creamed corn into a baking dish then top with the breadcrumb mixture. Broil for 2 to 3 minutes until the topping is nicely browned. You can serve it immediately or at room temperature.

# BACON GREEN BEANS

This is a well-known dish in the South, and for good reason. The green beans get very soft and the salty bacon adds the perfect crunch. Even people who have claimed they don't care for green beans change their minds when I serve them this dish!

**YIELD: 4 SERVINGS**

6 slices bacon, sliced crosswise into ½-inch (1.3-cm) pieces

¼ medium onion, chopped

½ cup (118 ml) chicken broth

1 (32-oz [908-g]) bag frozen green beans

2 tbsp (28 g) unsalted butter, softened

1 tsp coarse salt

½ tsp freshly ground black pepper

1 large pinch red pepper flakes (optional)

Press "Saute" to preheat your Instant Pot. When the word "Hot" appears on the display, add the bacon and cook until it's browned and crispy. Remove the bacon with a slotted spoon and place it on paper towels to absorb the excess grease. Add the onion to the bacon drippings in the pot. Cook until it's soft, for about 5 minutes, stirring frequently. Turn off the Instant Pot.

Add the chicken broth, stirring well to scrape up any browned bits from the bottom. Add the green beans to the pot. Close and lock the lid of the Instant Pot. Press "Manual" and immediately adjust the timer to 10 minutes. Check that the cooking pressure is on "High" and that the release valve is set to "Sealing."

When the time is up, open the Instant Pot using "Quick Pressure Release." Add the butter, salt, pepper, red pepper flakes (if using) and the reserved bacon to the beans and gently toss.

# CHEESY BROCCOLI MASH

This delightful dish was the result of a happy accident! While I was testing broccoli recipes for this book, I decided to mash a batch that I'd overcooked when I realized that it would be delicious with some milk and cheese mixed in. It's a wonderful way to introduce picky eaters to broccoli too!

**YIELD: 4 SERVINGS**

¼ cup (59 ml) chicken broth

1 (32-oz [908-g]) bag frozen broccoli florets

3 tbsp (43 g) butter

1 cup (236 ml) whole milk

1 cup (113 g) freshly grated sharp cheddar cheese

Coarse salt and freshly ground black pepper

Add the chicken broth and broccoli to the pot. Close and lock the lid of the Instant Pot. Press "Manual" and immediately adjust the timer to 3 minutes. Check that the cooking pressure is on "High" and that the release valve is set to "Sealing."

When the time is up, open the Instant Pot using "Quick Pressure Release." Add the butter and milk to the pot. Mash the broccoli with a potato masher to your desired consistency. Stir in the cheese until it's melted. Season with salt and pepper.

# PARMESAN CORN OVER BROILED RICOTTA

This might be my favorite side dish in this book. It's so simple with a wonderful texture and flavor, yet it's elegant enough to serve to company.

**YIELD: 4 SERVINGS**

2 tbsp (28 g) butter

2 cloves garlic, minced

¼ cup (59 ml) chicken broth

3 cups (492 g) frozen corn

2 tbsp (30 ml) heavy cream

2 cups (230 g) whole-milk ricotta cheese

1 tsp coarse salt

Freshly ground black pepper

¼ cup (25 g) grated Parmesan cheese

2 tbsp (5 g) chopped basil

Press "Saute" to preheat your Instant Pot. When the word "Hot" appears on the display, add the butter. When the butter is almost melted, add the garlic and cook for about 1 minute. Turn off the Instant Pot.

Add the chicken broth, stirring well to scrape up any browned bits from the bottom. Add the corn to the pot.

Close and lock the lid of the Instant Pot. Press "Manual" and immediately adjust the timer to 1 minute. Check that the cooking pressure is on "High" and that the release valve is set to "Sealing."

Meanwhile, mix together the cream, ricotta, salt and pepper. Place it in a shallow, broiler-proof baking dish. Sprinkle with Parmesan cheese. Broil until the cheese is lightly browned.

When the time is up, open the Instant Pot using "Quick Pressure Release." Remove the corn with a slotted spoon and spread it on top of the broiled ricotta. Top with the fresh basil.

*See photo on page 158.

# BLUE CHEESE GREEN BEAN CASSEROLE

You'll love the twist of blue cheese in this green bean casserole! Chopping French fried onions and mixing them with panko breadcrumbs also adds flavor with the perfect texture for the tender, creamy green beans. I serve this often at holiday gatherings and once you try it, I bet you will too!

**YIELD: 6 TO 8 SERVINGS**

½ cup (114 g) unsalted butter, divided

1 large onion, chopped

2 cloves garlic, minced

½ cup (118 ml) chicken broth

1 (32-oz [908-g]) bag frozen green beans

2 tbsp (16 g) cornstarch

2 tbsp (30 ml) cold water

1½ cups (354 ml) heavy cream

½ cup (76 g) crumbled blue cheese

1 tsp coarse salt

1 cup (226 g) French fried onions, chopped

1 cup (108 g) panko breadcrumbs

Press "Saute" to preheat your Instant Pot. When the word "Hot" appears on the display, add ¼ cup (57 g) of the butter. When the butter is almost melted, add the onion. Cook until it's soft, for about 5 minutes, stirring frequently. Add the garlic and cook for 1 minute. Turn off the Instant Pot.

Add the chicken broth, stirring well to scrape up any browned bits from the bottom. Add the green beans to the pot. Close and lock the lid of the Instant Pot. Press "Manual" and immediately adjust the timer to 5 minutes. Check that the cooking pressure is on "High" and that the release valve is set to "Sealing."

When the time is up, open the Instant Pot using "Quick Pressure Release." Press "Cancel," then "Saute." Mix together the cornstarch and water. When the liquid in the pot is at a strong simmer, add the cornstarch "slurry." Stir continually for at least a minute until it's thickened. Add the cream, blue cheese and salt to the pot, stirring until the blue cheese starts to soften and melt.

Pour the blue cheese mixture into a baking dish. Mix together the French fried onions and breadcrumbs. Melt the remaining ¼ cup (57 g) of butter and mix it in with the breadcrumb mixture. Spread it over the top of the casserole.

Broil until the casserole topping is nicely browned, for about 6 to 8 minutes.

*See photo on page 3.

# CURRIED RICE AND VEGGIES

This side dish is so simple and versatile with a wonderful flavor that will complement any Indian-inspired meal! Feel free to add frozen chicken tenders at step two for a meat main dish, or you can serve this as a vegetarian main dish with a side salad.

## YIELD: 6 SERVINGS

2 tbsp (28 g) unsalted butter

1 large sweet onion, chopped

4 cloves garlic, minced

1 tsp curry powder

¼ tsp turmeric

2½ cups (590 ml) low-sodium chicken broth

1 tbsp (15 ml) fresh lemon juice

1 cinnamon stick

2 cups (370 g) brown basmati rice

1 (12-oz [340-g]) bag frozen mixed vegetables

¼ cup (10 g) chopped fresh cilantro

Press "Saute" to preheat your Instant Pot. When the word "Hot" appears on the display, add the butter. When the butter is almost melted, add the onion. Cook until it's soft, for about 5 minutes, stirring frequently. Add the garlic, curry powder and turmeric and cook for 1 minute. Turn off the Instant Pot.

Add the chicken broth, stirring well to scrape up any browned bits from the bottom. Add the lemon juice, cinnamon stick, rice and veggies to the pot. Close and lock the lid of the Instant Pot. Press "Manual" and immediately adjust the timer to 22 minutes. Check that the cooking pressure is on "High" and that the release valve is set to "Sealing."

When the time is up, open the Instant Pot using "Quick Pressure Release." Discard the cinnamon stick, then fluff the rice with a fork and top with the cilantro.

# MUSHY PEAS WITH FRESH MINT

If you like peas, you must try this recipe! You won't believe the flavor it has from such a short list of ingredients. I've been known to polish off an entire batch of this in one sitting. The Instant Pot is perfect since you can have your hands free while assembling the remaining ingredients, making quick work of a delicious side dish.

**YIELD: 4 SERVINGS**

¼ cup (59 ml) chicken broth

1 (12-oz [340-g]) bag frozen peas

¼ cup (59 ml) heavy cream

2 tbsp (28 g) unsalted butter

1 tsp coarse salt

¼ tsp freshly ground black pepper

1 tbsp (2.5 g) chopped fresh mint

Add the chicken broth to the pot, then add the peas.

Close and lock the lid of the Instant Pot. Press "Manual" and immediately adjust the timer to 1 minute. Check that the cooking pressure is on "High" and that the release valve is set to "Sealing."

When the time is up, open the pot using "Quick Pressure Release." Press "Cancel," then immediately press "Saute." Add the cream and butter, stirring occasionally until the butter is melted. Using a potato masher, mash the peas until about half are smooth and the rest crushed. Stir in the salt, pepper and mint.

# CHIPOTLE AND BLACK BEAN POTATO SALAD

Whenever I take this salad to a picnic, it's always the first thing gone and I get endless requests for the recipe. People are always surprised when they see black beans in a potato salad, but they go so well with the chipotle and poblano flavors and make for a deliciously different Mexican side dish.

### YIELD: 4 TO 6 SERVINGS

1½ cups (354 ml) low-sodium chicken broth

1 lb (454 g) frozen chipotle-flavored or andouille sausage

1½ lb (680 g) red potatoes, halved (or quartered if large)

1 cup (230 g) mayonnaise

¼ medium red onion, diced

3 chipotle peppers, chopped

1 poblano pepper, chopped

½ red bell pepper, chopped

1 (15-oz [425-g]) can black beans, rinsed and drained

4 hard-boiled eggs, chopped

¼ cup (10 g) chopped cilantro

1 tsp coarse salt

Freshly ground black pepper

Pour the chicken broth, sausage and potatoes into the bottom of the pot. Close and lock the lid of the Instant Pot. Press "Manual" and immediately adjust the timer to 15 minutes. Check that the cooking pressure is on "High" and that the release valve is set to "Sealing."

Meanwhile, mix together the mayonnaise, onion, peppers, beans, eggs, cilantro and salt and pepper and set it aside.

When the time is up, open the Instant Pot using "Quick Pressure Release." Carefully remove the sausage and potatoes and set them aside to cool slightly, then toss them with the dressing mixture.

# CREAMY GARLIC PARMESAN RICE

This simple, flavorful side dish goes with almost any main dish you're serving. I especially love it with the Honey Mustard–Glazed Pork Rib Roast (page 66). Like the Curried Rice and Veggies (page 165), you can add some frozen chicken tenders, and it becomes an easy main dish too!

**YIELD: 4 TO 6 SERVINGS**

2 tbsp (28 g) unsalted butter

¼ medium onion, chopped

4 cloves garlic, minced

¼ cup (59 ml) dry white wine

1 cup (236 ml) low-sodium chicken broth

1 cup (185 g) white rice, rinsed

½ cup (118 ml) heavy cream

¼ cup (25 g) grated Parmesan cheese

½ tsp salt

Freshly ground black pepper

2 tbsp (5 g) chopped fresh parsley

Press "Saute" to preheat your Instant Pot. When the word "Hot" appears on the display, add the butter. When the butter is almost melted, add the onion. Cook until it's soft, about 5 minutes, stirring frequently. Add the garlic and cook for 1 minute. Add the wine, stirring to scrape up any browned bits from the bottom of the pot, and cook until the wine has almost completely evaporated, about 3 to 4 minutes. Turn off the Instant Pot.

Add the chicken broth and rice to the pot. Close and lock the lid. Press "Manual" and immediately adjust the timer to 3 minutes. Check that the cooking pressure is on "High" and that the release valve is set to "Sealing."

When the time is up, allow the pressure to release naturally. Stir in the cream, Parmesan cheese, salt and pepper. Top with the parsley.

# ACKNOWLEDGMENTS

Thank you to the following people:

Mom and Dad, without whom this book wouldn't be possible. You make everything in life so much sweeter.

My girls, Kylie and Katie, who bring joy to my world every day.

For my publisher and team, who believed in me enough to sign me for a second book!

Rob, my taste tester and BFF.

Lara, for your laughter and for always having a listening ear. You are all that's good in the world!

# ABOUT THE AUTHOR

Kristy Bernardo is the author of *Weeknight Cooking with Your Instant Pot®* and the creator of the popular food blog The Wicked Noodle. Although mostly self-taught, she has been strongly influenced by her mother and grandmother and honed her skills at boot camp at the Culinary Institute of America in Hyde Park, NY. She has owned a successful business as a personal chef, has taught cooking classes to all ages, speaks at conferences and events and has appeared regularly on video and television. Her work as both a food and travel writer has appeared in many mainstream online publications, such as the *Huffington Post*, *Food & Wine* magazine, *Better Homes and Gardens* and many more.

Kristy lives in northern Virginia with her two daughters, Kylie and Katie, and their two cats, Mr. Pepper and Princess Whiskers. You can most often find her walking the nearby trails, riding her motorcycle in Virginia's gorgeous wine country or trying new dishes and cocktails at restaurants everywhere.

# INDEX